Welcome to Heaven

Your Graduation from Kindergarten Earth School to Heaven

Trinity Royal

© **Copyright 2022 - All rights reserved.**

The content contained within this book may not be reproduced, duplicated, or transmitted without direct written permission from the author or the publisher. Under no circumstances will any blame or legal responsibility be held against the publisher, or author, for any damages, reparation, or monetary loss due to the information contained within this book, either directly or indirectly.

Legal Notice: This book is copyright protected. It is only for personal use. You cannot amend, distribute, sell, use, quote, or paraphrase any part, or the content within this book, without the consent of the author or publisher.

Disclaimer Notice: Please note the information contained within this document is for educational and entertainment purposes only. All effort has been executed to present accurate, up-to-date, reliable, and complete information. No warranties of any kind are declared or implied. Readers acknowledge that the author is not engaged in the rendering of legal, financial, medical or professional advice. The content within this book has been derived from various sources. Please consult a licensed professional before attempting any techniques outlined in this book.

Library of Congress Control Number: 2023906291 | Digital ISBN: 978-1-957681-21-4

Contents

Free books to our readers i
Introduction iv
The Roadmap 1
Does Heaven Exist? 7
What is the Meaning of Life? 25
Heaven Around the World 36
How does One go to Heaven? Are there any Minimum Requirements? 51
Understanding Earth as a Kindergarten School 65
What is the Graduation Process from Kindergarten to First Grade? 79
The Various Levels of Heaven 95
Is there Graduation and Post-Graduation in Heavenly School? 111
Questions and Answers 127
The Advantages of Being on Earth's School 140
Conclusion 162
Thank You 167

Preview Chapter from book 2 of series Welcome to Heaven. Your Family, Marriage, Sex, Work 168
References 213
About Author 217

FREE BOOKS TO OUR READERS

War in Heaven came to Earth. Satan Rebellion:

https://dl.bookfunnel.com/ea12ys3dmk

Your Life in Heaven:

https://dl.bookfunnel.com/vg451qpuzs

> For what will it profit a man if he gains the whole world and forfeits his soul?
>
> – Mark 8:36

"Seek first the kingdom of God above all else"- Mark 6:53

Introduction

The idea of Heaven has been a part of the human experience for millennia. Since early ages, people have yearned for a place that offers something far better than what earthly experiences have to offer. Life has always been hard. Thousands of years ago, people struggled to find enough food and shelter for themselves. The bigger difficulties of life were about conquering nature and learning how to survive in a harsh world/environment. Earth seemed harsher, and humans needed to find ways to be more hopeful for the future.

In contemporary society, despite technological advancements that have made the struggles for food and shelter largely obsolete for most of the modern world, humanity is still grappling with some massive challenges. The complexities of this world, the conflicting narratives of truth, the difficulties of mental health, and the overall state of the world today have made people feel even less content with life than our ancestors. Over the years, people have struggled to find meaning, purpose, and fulfillment in life. Earth has always been a cruel and difficult place for people to live in.

What, then, is the real solution?

This book will clarify what is to be done in regard to escaping the problems of this dead-end world and will help people start on their journeys toward a truer, deeper experience... one that we know as Heaven.

The purpose of writing this book is to bring Heaven a little closer to you and to de-mystify Heaven to some extent. I wish to make Heaven as much tangible as possible in these pages.

This book is written for those who are seeking to acquire knowledge to either create a new faith or empower their existing devotion to embrace God, the One Infinite Creator who abides in Heaven, and to bring Him closer in our daily lives.

Earth is Your Kinder-Garden School

A good foundation is required to be able to advance in your heavenly journey. This solid foundation is only possible at the lowest level. Earthly life is truly our Kindergarten school level.

If you were to learn a completely new language, one you had never spoken before, you might be very pleased if you could read a book at the level of a kindergartner. Someone who has just learned to read can try their best to sound out the words, the new letters and shapes make sense but only on a basic level. Also, your reading comprehension is very limited. You probably only understand basic shapes, colors, numbers, and maybe a few animals.

Please keep this in mind when reading this book as a guide to graduating from the kindergarten of Earth and entering into the first-grade level of Heaven. This is not meant to be an insulting or belittling framework, but rather an honest one. Even if you have some ideas about the religious constructs of Heaven, the reality of what Heaven is, and how you can get there, it is likely not beyond what was explained in Sunday School.

You wouldn't start educating a child at a university nor would you begin to directly learn about Heaven from an advanced level. You are, for all intents and purposes, new to this subject matter, and so you need an introduction that will meet you where you currently are, so that your knowledge can grow against a solid foundation of understanding.

With that understanding, please be patient with yourself, and understand that you are exploring the truths of this Earth and of the factual Heaven that you hope to join one day. Like any kindergartener who is learning to read, it will take time, patience, and you may not always understand a few things. That is completely okay. Take your time and read this as many times as you need until you grasp the meaning of what is being shared with you. Then, when you are ready, you can take further steps into seeing and experiencing the realities of Heaven.

It is important to approach the information in this book with the right amount of humility. While topics like Heaven, the Bible, and salvation may sound familiar to some, they have often not been framed correctly by modern Christianity.

In this book, you will learn the absolute basics: the foundational building blocks about the reality of Heaven, the meaning of life, the value of pursuing an eternity in Heaven, a perspective of our time on Earth as an educational stepping stone, graduating from the earthly plane, the advancements in Heaven, what your time on Earth can be valuable for, and how you can improve your knowledge to be able to successfully navigate the spiritual questions around Heaven, Earth, and your place within the spiritual realms.

The good news is that everyone has opportunities to come to this knowledge. You do not have to be of a particular religious background to find truth and value in what you are about to explore. Anyone, no matter how old or young, can benefit from the knowledge and wisdom imparted through these pages. The more student-like attitude you have, the easier your journey can become. By reading this guide, you are taking the very first step in a series of baby steps that will ultimately lead to your coming to graduate toward the beginning of your future heavenly experience.

What to Expect from This Book

The idea of the deceased in Heaven or enjoying paradise can bring enormous comfort to the bereaved as well as hope to those who are suffering or facing death. The purpose of writing this book is to bring Heaven that little bit closer to you and make Heaven as much tangible as possible while having a human experience.

This book is written out of inspiration. Its purpose is to raise conscious awareness of God,

Christ, and Creation in general. While it is also written to fuel education for daily Christians, it is from the viewpoint that anyone who wants to know more about God, the son of God, and Heaven can discover information and insight among these pages. If you have picked up this book, it is not necessary to have a background in Christian theology but to have an open mind and heart while reading.

The chapters will describe and uncover the mysteries of this sacred place called Heaven and attempt to answer the many dubious questions around it. It will clarify many ideas surrounding this mystical place that has eluded doubters for centuries and explore the concepts of soul and spirit with references from the Bible, mystics, and other schools of religious and spiritual thought.

Through my own understanding and these references, I will attempt to answer questions you may have that may not be available or clearly defined in other literature, and I welcome you on this journey of exploration.

Once you understand the basics of Heaven in these next chapters, you yourself will be able to answer many questions that you may have including:

- *Isn't Heaven just a mind concept? What is the proof of its existence? Is there biblical evidence?*

- *Why do I even bother about Heaven? What is in it for me?*

- *What are the minimum requirements to go to Heaven or the ticket booth to Heaven?*

- *What exactly is Soul?*

- *What exactly is Spirit? What does born of spirit mean?*

- *What are the main constituents of humans in the material world other than our physical bodies?*

- *Why is life on Earth our kindergarten school?*

- *Are there different levels to heaven? If so, how many? What are they?*

- *Does the time and space continuum exist in Heaven? If so how different is it compared to Earth's time and space?*

- *What body will you have in heaven?*

- *Where will you go when you die?*

- *What happens to all our life experiences, including successes, failures, shortcomings, and illnesses after death?*

- *Why life on Earth is so difficult? Why is God/Christ not waving a magic wand and resolving all problems?*

THE ROADMAP

First and foremost, this book will talk about Heaven. For the many believers of this Eternal Kingdom, what do we really know about it? The following chapters will provide an overview of what we know about Heaven from the Bible and other resources and explore why in the hearts and minds of followers of Christ and God there exists the intrinsic desire to go to Heaven. But why is this place so incredibly uncertain? There are many clues scattered in the scriptures and across various other references that, once pieced together, paint an idea of what this picture-perfect place is, and that will allow its miraculous impressions to become embedded more clearly in our minds. The idea of Heaven is well-known, and most people have a general idea of what it entails. But even Christ did not give many details about what Heaven exactly is.

Chapter-2: Does Heaven Exist?

- We will look at some of the scriptural evidence related to Heaven.

- What does Bible say about heaven, its structure, levels to heaven, and how many angels are there?
- Also what exactly did Christ say about the kingdom of Heaven
- Common misconceptions about heaven

Chapter-3: Meaning of Life

- What is the purpose and meaning of life?
- Is there a connection between being alive to heaven?
- How does the birth of the spirit occur and its relation to the breath of life?
- God's purpose in creating you and me.
- God pull vs gravitational pull.

Chapter-4: Heaven – Is it worth it?

- Why Heaven, is it worth it?
- Is there a reason for you and me to consider Heaven?
- What do different religions say about Heaven?

Chapter-5: How does one go to Heaven? Are there any minimum requirements?

- What is the general process for any person to go to Heaven?
- What are the absolute minimum requirements to have a ticket to Heaven?
- What is a Soul?
- What are the consequences for those who do not meet the minimum requirements?
- What does "born of the spirit" mean?

Chapter-6: Understanding Earth as a Kindergarten School.

- Why do we consider earth life as a foundation for Heavenly eternal life?
- Why is there so much evil and trauma and sorrow on earth?
- What exactly is Lucifer Rebellion and its effects on Earth and Human life?
- Why planet Earth has unique opportunities, that even angels in heaven do not have?
- Why does God not use a magic wand to remove all evil?
- What are we expected to learn in this Kindergarten school of the earth?

- How big is the spiral ladder of evolution?
- Can you skip levels and graduate to higher levels of Heaven?

Chapter-7: What is the Graduation Process from Kindergarten to First Grade?

- What are the minimum requirements for graduation to the first level of Heaven?
- What exactly happens after a person dies? What happens to the person's Spirit and Soul?
- What does eternal life mean? Is there a resurrection process? If so what is it, and how does it happen?
- How did Christ's Resurrection process happen? Are there any similarities?

Chapter-8: The various levels of Heaven

- What is the structure of Heaven? How many levels are there generally?
- How do time and space work in different levels of Heaven?

Chapter-9: Is there graduation and post-graduation from Heavenly School?

- If there are multiple levels, there are also multiple graduations; How does one graduate from lower level to higher levels of Heaven?
- What exactly happens at higher levels of the graduation process (conceptualize college graduation and post-graduation)?
- What happens to one's Soul and Spirit during this graduation process?

Chapter-11: Answering Your Questions

- As a recap, we will answer all the above questions explicitly in this chapter.

Chapter-11: The Advantages of Earth School

- Why the life on earth is very difficult and mostly sorrow filled?
- Why do God and Angels consider you a Superhero when you are able to graduate from Earth?
- Most Superheroes have a dark past that makes them who they are. How does this relate to present Earth conditions?
- Life on earth is very short compared to eternal life. Like a water bubble or like a vapor that vanishes at dawn,

make the best use of the time you have on Earth.

- Why do God and Christ offer more than extra grace and mercy to earthlings?
- What does "Last shall be the first and first shall be the last" mean?

DOES HEAVEN EXIST?

Many people, over the centuries, have tried to approach this question through various means. Some have tried to prove it scientifically by understanding the matter of the universe. Scientific lenses, while useful in many ways, can only operate with an earthly understanding of the relationship between physical mass, anti-mass, and forces such as gravity. They do not sufficiently take into account spiritual realms that could only be truly known and experienced through religious understandings. On the other hand, some others have tried to come to know Heaven spiritually by attempting to transcend planes. This is very difficult and has rarely been achieved. Most people do not have a proper guide or the right orientation when they pursue this way to go beyond this earthly world and temporal realms, and into the heavenly realms.

This all results in many people attaining a false Heaven, or not understanding Heaven, or flat-out denying the existence of Heaven. The number of skeptics in the world today is on the rise, and, to be honest, it is not hard to understand why. With Heaven being virtually invisible to human senses—and without proper religious guidance and teachings that can direct someone to a real experience of what Heaven will be—humans have so rarely been able to get a real glimpse of Heaven that they often easily give up and declare that it is foolish to engage in believing in such a place.

Coming to the right understanding and perspective on Heaven is not easy, and it is not a pursuit that should be taken lightly. It takes dedication and a willingness to learn, and especially to challenge one's preconceived notions to reach a meaningful view of the reality of Heaven's existence.

Firstly, you must understand your starting point. Are you a scientific skeptic? Are you a devout Christian who has never had a proper understanding of Heaven? Are you someone who has tried many religions and is looking for the right one? Regardless of how you identify, it is important that you now see yourself as a curious beginner looking for the truth revealed in the image of Jesus Christ alone. Remember the framework from the introduction that this is a kindergarten, and, like a child, you will need to learn the world around you with brand new eyes. What may seem familiar to you will need to be seen in new ways if you are intending to fully grasp the depth of the relationship between this Earth and the eternal Heaven.

Biblical Evidence

Throughout the Bible, there is ample evidence that supports the reality of Heaven. In Hebrew scriptures found in the Old Testament, there is some scant evidence, but it becomes clarified in New Testament Scriptures, especially through the words of Jesus himself. We will explore a few here:

The first time that the word "Heaven" appears in the *Bible* is in Genesis 1:1 "In the beginning, God created the Heaven and the earth." The first chapter of the Bible conveys to us that God's creation of Heaven happened simultaneously with God's creation of Earth. The Earth is evidently real. We live here, we see it, we interact with one another on Earth, and no one doubts the existence of this planet, so we ought to realize that this suggests the parallel statement must also be true. God did create Heaven and the earth. Earth, as we know, is real, and therefore Heaven must also be.

More than that, however, by beginning with the act of creating Heaven, scripture shows us that this is the priority of God. The first thing God does in the act of creation is to make Heaven. From that starting point, the rest of the Bible orients itself between these two realms. The earthly and the temporal realm, and the eternal heavenly realm. In dozens of books of the *Bible*, there are countless references to Heaven and to God's desire for humanity to move toward attaining that very Heaven.

Psalm 115 reads as follows: "The highest Heavens belong to the LORD, but the earth He has given to man." Of course, this makes sense if we think of Earth as being removed from God. We can look around and clearly see that this is not Heaven. Therefore, knowing that Heaven was also created at the same time as Earth, we know that Heaven must be somewhere else, too. By clarifying this in the Psalms, there is the reassurance that although our scientific methods cannot locate Heaven in our understanding of the physical plane, the heavenly realm is something else entirely and just belongs to God.

John 18:36 tells us the words of Christ when he reiterates, "My kingdom is not of this world." These words are spoken in response to Pontious Pilate who has put Jesus on trial. While the Pharisees, Sadducees, and Romans are trying to trap Jesus into claiming an earthly kingdom, which would put him at odds with the Roman Empire as well as the Hebrew Temple, Jesus sidesteps their snare by clarifying that the kingdom that Jesus has dominion over is not a part of this world.

In 2 Corinthians, Paul writes about a "third Heaven" while discussing the realities of the eternal with his readers.

With this knowledge of Heaven existing outside of our earthly understanding, we can start to see a clearer picture of what Heaven is and is not. In 2 Corinthians 12:4, and in Revelations 2:7, Heaven is referred to as "Paradise." We will look into what this may mean at a later stage.

Heaven is referred to as "My Father's house" by Jesus in John 14:2, an "eternal inheritance" in 1 Peter 1:4, and is where Jesus goes to prepare a place for those who are his followers. If we are wondering who is already there, Revelation 5:11-13 tells us that there will be "thousands upon thousands, and ten thousand times ten thousand" angels occupying the heavenly realms.

Philippians 3:20-21 clarifies that true citizenship for the believers in Christ is not found on any earthly registry, but purely belongs to Heaven. Similarly, Paul shares that what is heavenly is of a purer, more enduring, substance than that which we can know on Earth.

These are just a few of several examples of biblical references to Heaven.

Deductions on Biblical Evidence

All references to Heaven that we come to read in the *Bible* are layered on top of one another. We know that they are true because we read how they complement one another and are not in contradiction. We see consistent evidence of the reality of the word of God in the *Bible* as it plays out in this earthly existence. It, therefore, only makes sense if we realize that God's Word is also the truth when it attempts to reveal the reality and nature of Heaven to us.

Multiple interpretations about Heaven will only divide and confuse us. Oftentimes, popular culture can paint a false picture of Heaven, too. Similarly, those who pursue their own understanding of Heaven can digress from the biblical tradition, and end up with complicated contradictions that reveal their teachings to be false. At the most basic level, we know that Heaven is real and does exist because of the evidence provided in many scriptures that attest to God's creation of Heaven and Jesus' Kingdom.

What do we know from biblical evidence alone? We know that Heaven exists not as a concept of the mind, but as an actual physical location, a dwelling place, even if that location is beyond the scope of what we can perceive with our human senses and scientific advancements. We are also aware that the consistent references to Heaven as eternal, it reassures us that this is a place that will last forever and will be worth our efforts to finally reach it. It is a far better place that is ought to be looked forward to.

Based on Paul's words, we know that there are, at least, three levels of Heaven. This will be explored more fully later, but for now, it is enough to know that Heaven is complex, and the way that it is structured is beyond a basic idea of a simple realm.

We understand that Heaven is God's house and that there are many mansions and levels within the Heavenly realms. All of it, though, clearly belongs to Christ. Christ is the one who is the ruler of this kingdom, and we know that every kingdom has subjects, organizations, order, and structures that are overseen by the ruler. With Christ as king, we can presume, by the words he records in the gospels, what his kingdom will be (or is) like.

We know a little bit about the nature of Heaven as well, including the fact that there are an infinite number of angels in Heaven, and that varying levels have different substances of purity that endure differently than anything we can conceptualize on Earth. Most importantly, though, we know that it is possible for us to become citizens of this Heaven, and that comes with many rights and a sense of belonging... only if we recognize how to get there by following Christ's words, works, and examples.

Kingdom of Earth vs. the Kingdom of Heaven

Consistently, throughout the gospel texts, we read about Jesus telling his listeners about the Kingdom of Heaven, and describing what it is like and how to better know it through the parables and stories of His teachings.

To reiterate from an earlier argument, we know that Jesus tells Pilate that his kingdom is not of this world. He goes on to say, "if it were, my servants would fight that I should not be delivered to the Jews but now is my kingdom not from hence."

Countless parables also attest to the idea that the Kingdom of Heaven is not from here. Jesus tells us that the Kingdom of Heaven is like a mustard seed, a treasure in the field, a man buying pearls, a fisherman's net being dragged into the sea, a scattering of seed on various types of soil, a king who gives a wedding feast for his son, a landowner who hires day workers for his vineyard, and even more.

But how could the Kingdom of Heaven be like these things? Jesus clarifies this in Luke 8, when he says, "To you, it has been granted to know the mysteries of the kingdom of God, but to the rest, it is in parables so that seeing they may not see, and hearing they may not understand."

Therefore, these parables are meant for those who do not see the truth so that they may understand more clearly. It is okay if you do not see at first. The words of Jesus' parables can enlighten you with a deeper understanding of what the Kingdom of God is like. More than that, Jesus is also saying that there are those to whom the mystery has already been revealed. They do not need parables to see or to know the Kingdom of God. Jesus has offered them a sacred sight already so that the mysteries are known to them and the parables are no longer necessary.

At first, it sounds reassuring to know that Jesus spends so much of his speech on this Kingdom of Heaven only so that we may develop a greater understanding of it. Jesus even translates the mysteries into parables so that those who may not be granted special wisdom may attain the knowledge needed to get into Heaven. While this all sounds good, there is a startling question at the end of this line of reasoning.

If Jesus' kingdom is, indeed, Heaven, and if Jesus wants us to get here, further proof of what we already know; that Heaven is not of this Earthly realm, then the question remains - Who is the ruler of the Kingdom of Earth?

Satan, or the Evil One, rules over Earth. Is it any wonder then that this planet is so full of hatred, suffering, and death? Those are not from God, and thus this world is not God's world. This world is just a training ground, a kind of kindergarten, if we are going to continue the metaphor, so that we may one day graduate toward the heavenly eternal realms.

Questions on Kingdoms of Heaven and Earth

Understandably, most people have no interest in staying in the sphere of Satan's influence. We would rather get off the Earth and into Heaven. This would yield many questions, however: Where is Christ's Kingdom? Who is there? What does it look like and how can we get there? Are there any qualifications needed to get in and, if so, what are they? What are the rules that must be obeyed in order for the Kingdom to be good and worthy of the eternal promise given to us? If

Christ's kingdom is somewhere else, why did he come to Earth in the first place?

On top of these, do we know why Christ came to Earth? If it was a mission for Him, what was that mission? Was Christ here to wage a war against evil, or doing so was His will to liberate humans trapped in the veil of forgetfulness?

You may have some inkling of the answers to these questions from the biblical evidence we have already reviewed. The rest of the answers will be forthcoming, but it is important to note them here as we examine the relationship between the Kingdom of Earth vis-à-vis the Kingdom of Heaven.

As people who have previously believed we were citizens of Earth, but who now know that there is a citizenship of belonging that is reserved in the Kingdom of Heaven, these questions are all about the relationship between the two Kingdoms and how we can make sense of the Kingdom of Heaven and our migration from our current place to the eternal one.

Common Misconceptions

Before we enter into a chance to get into what the Kingdom of Heaven really is and develop an understanding of the relationship between the world we occupy now and the one we hope to achieve, we will need to dispel some rumors about what you may have believed about Heaven before reading this book.

It is important that we enter this knowledge with a clean slate. A true kindergartner does not have any preconceived notions of what numbers or letters or shapes or colors are. They do not have to *unlearn* to be taught properly. This is, however, not a luxury that we can afford. The following are three of the biggest misconceptions about Heaven. We must address them here and discard them from our mental constructs if we are to have any hope of one day being able to live into the reality of Heaven that is to come to us.

Misconception 1: Heaven will be Filled with Earthly Pleasures

This is a feature of many Hollywood tropes as well as religious follies.

Many times, people recognize that they are denied the good things in this world. People go through life unhappily and see their neighbors around them able to achieve more, being able to enjoy more and be more generally satisfied with this world. These fulfillments are about earthly pleasures. Extravagance, wealth, and, at times, sexual gratification, have all been seen as desires to be attained on Earth.

When people do not experience them on Earth, they want to believe in a Heaven that gives them an opportunity to enjoy what they could not experience on earth.

If your motivation for Heaven is pleasure and desire, you are not willing to see the depths of the spiritual realms. If a movie is showing Heaven as indulgent of the worst of earthly gluttons, it is certainly not Heaven. Similarly, if a religion promises the joys of the flesh to be fulfilled in the heavenly realm, they are simply playing on your earthly desires without respect for any biblical teachings that will help you to realize the deeper meanings of spiritual fulfillment.

Please, leave these easy and simple ways of looking at Heaven behind. Although it may be difficult to divorce yourself from this concept of Heaven - who, after all, does not want to feel fulfilled? - the true greatness of the eternal realms will be far better than any sort of earthly desires that you may be able to conceive of.

Misconception 2: Everyone who is Good Shall go to Heaven

This one is hard because many people want to be assured that their loved ones will attain the heavenly realm. This may be possible for them. After all, God is good and God has given the blueprint to us through Jesus Christ so that we may be able to come to know the wholeness of Heaven. It is not, however, an absolute promise.

Plenty of people who have been deemed "good" by our modern understanding of ethics and morals have not been able to grasp the necessary knowledge that would help them to graduate from this world into the heavenly realm.

Our understanding of what is good and evil is based on a religious framework that has been given to us in the *Bible*. So, while we know that we must be good to one day attain Heaven, simply being considered good is not in itself enough to release someone from this earthly plane.

This is not to say that being good is useless in pursuing a transition from Earth to Heaven. One must be good in word, deed, and in the knowledge of the progress from this world to Christ's eternal Kingdom. Being good is just one step among many others that must be taken to graduate to Christ's heavenly abode.

Misconception 3: Heaven will be a Place from Where I can Watch my Loved Ones on Earth

This is another piece of media lore. Hollywood and popular culture are filled with stories of people dying, achieving a false idea of Heaven, and then looking back on, or, at times, even guiding their loved ones who are still on Earth.

When the reality of Heaven is achieved, the connection to physicality eventually gets slimmer and slimmer. There is however a period of grace that is granted to beings of this universe that Christ is a creator of. Christ's universe encourages relationships. Eventually, the physical reality is abandoned, and the true forms of soul and spirit are unlocked. In this way, the physical connections that we experience now between places and people that we love will also dissolve eventually.

Try not to think of this with sadness. In some sense, it can be difficult for people to think of Heaven without their loved ones. In another, it is important to realize that there is so much more greatness and fulfillment to your soul that you cannot conceive of through concepts of earthly love and connection. By releasing ourselves from our desire for incomplete love known between humans and realizing deeper realities of God's creation for us in the form of Heaven, our souls can infinitely experience feelings that are far more powerful and fulfilling than love.

Again, we must trust God's vision for Heaven and see Earth as only a kindergarten. If you think reading basic words and books is what matters the most, as a kindergartner might, you will miss the profound revelations known through reading and comprehending biblical texts. This is also the case with earthly love. Our basic understanding can only guide us as far as we are capable of understanding, but the heavenly realm will offer many more complexities, nuances, and a sense of completeness that we cannot imagine.

Misconception 4: Heaven is boring

The misconception is that when we go to Heaven, even though all is good and well there and it sounds nice, *what exactly is there to do*? Can we really just sit around listening to harps all day and gaze upon the heavenly clouds with compliant acceptance? When you come into a relationship with God and know that he is the Creator of Heaven and Earth, then quite realistically you will understand that he is not boring. In fact, quite the opposite. God has created our laughter, our funny bones, the adrenaline in our bodies, our taste buds, sensory experiences, and the excitement and passion for life that exists in the Heavens. As we will see in this book, there are many levels to Heaven, and you can have endless experiences as you desire.

WAT IS THE MEANING OF LIFE?

It's no secret that our ancestors struggled to live. Food, water, shelter, and many of the things we take for granted today, were not easily available and not all of them were safe options for people. Over time, as agriculture and culture developed, and peoples' life expectancy increased, they learned to view themselves in their position within the world... and eventually in the universe.

All of this brought with it several larger questions. When life was spent making sure that there was enough food to eat, there wasn't enough time to wonder about the purpose of that life. As advancements in the human experience allowed for more curiosity about life itself, it was natural to see people turn that question inward.

What is the meaning of life?

This is a great question for philosophy. Ever since the ancient Greeks, people have attempted to find or make meaning out of this life. We, humans, are uniquely aware of our existence. Other animals do not have the capacity to question, wonder, create art or meaning, or have thoughts beyond basic survival instincts. It is natural, then, to wonder why that is so.

Although ancient Greek philosophers tried to answer, as have many other philosophers since then, they all fall short, especially because their answers do not align with Jesus Christ's life and teachings. Any answer to the question of the meaning of life that does not incorporate God is not a true or whole answer that is required of such a profound and invaluable question.

It is a question not to be asked idly and not to be wondered for the mere sake of curiosity either. If you are truly seeking the meaning of life, then you should also be seeking a way to reorient your life around the answer. The difficult but necessary next step is taking what you learn and applying it to your life, even if it is uncomfortable or difficult to fulfill.

What are we learning then? Not just about the meaning of life, but how to live in a way that fulfills that meaning that we come to see more fully now in the light of God's Day.

The Meaning of Life

Now that we know that Heaven exists and that we have the opportunity to become citizens of that Heaven, there is already an inkling of what this life is all about. It isn't about making money or having fancy things. It isn't about having the most friends or being the most successful. It isn't about accruing knowledge or being the smartest in your field either. It isn't even about having a big family or close loved ones.

But, why not? Many of those things are how we define value in our lives today. How do we get it so wrong?

To answer those questions, let's take a look at what happens when we die. When we die, our bodies shut down. Our brain stops sending signals to the body. Our heart stops pumping. Our breathing stops. It is interesting though that breathing is what controls our body's continued existence. Think about all of the medical dramas you may have seen on TV or in a CPR class you have taken. You are doing your best to keep the other person breathing, even by helping them to do so artificially. Without that, nothing else will work.

Birth of Spirit

When a person is born, the mortal and physical frame is guided by God's spark of consciousness. The essence that comes from God is then imbued in what is called Spirit, or breath of life. Each person's breathing possesses God's essence or the spark of God's creative consciousness.

This is because the Spirit within us gives us the breath of life. When God (in Hebrew) YHWH gives Adam life, He does so by breathing into him. Some Talmudic scholars even believe that the Hebrew word "YHWH" is just four breath sounds. Maybe, the very name of God is simply breathing.

In this way, every living person carries with them the divine spark. If you have breath in your lungs, you have it because God has used His own breath to give it to you. This is precisely the meaning of the phrase, "You are born in the image of God."

The Spirit resides in you, gently guiding you and helping you to reach to your full potential. This gift of personality is a glimpse of the consciousness of God. In this way, you are made in the image of God, as it says across the scriptures.

This breath is the part of you that connects you with the eternal. When your life ends, your breath does, too. You cannot continue to exist in this earthly world without the gift of God's breath. Therefore, being alive means having breath. Life is meant to be spent using these breaths for greater purposes than simply inhaling and exhaling. These breaths, the personality imbued by us, and the chance to reflect the very image of God is what our life is all about. If we spend our days and waste our breath on our own selfish motivations or try to fulfill ourselves through the ways of this world, we will have squandered the good gifts given to us and be left with nothing when the breath leaves our bodies for good.

What is God's Purpose of the Breath of Life in You and Me?

Now that we know that God's breath within us is the driving force of our life on Earth, we can finally approach the question through a proper lens. Instead of asking, "what is the meaning of life?" maybe it is more appropriate to ask, "what is God's purpose of giving the Breath of Life to you and me? Because the breath comes from God, it gives us a chance to hold on to the eternal divine that is within us and is part of God's creation here on Earth. The purpose, therefore, is to experience God's creation. Not just for ourselves alone. This is an opportunity for God to experience creation because God is in the breath we have. We are stewards of God, offering the Divine a tour of the creation of Earth. Each time we experience something new, we are also showing God a perspective of this creation.

This is precisely why vapid and shallow pursuits leave us feeling hollow. If we try to gain wealth, power, or influence, they do nothing for the 'Breath of God' within us. This is not to say to not pursue wealth or power but to use the same for

God's glory. God has more wealth, power, and influence than this earthly realm could ever imagine. In fact, God's ultimate power goes so far beyond any constraints of this world that it is laughable that we would try to find meaning in such pursuits. We become so caught up in our labels of good or bad, and our own social constructs, cultural creations, or earthly frameworks, that we forget how irrelevant they are to the God of all the Universe.

The idea of having a Spirit-filled existence is to enrich our life, or God's Spirit within us, by our experiences which will ultimately lead us to become one with God. This is the very essence of the journey for every spirit-infused mortal. The purpose of life is to offer the most positive experiences for the Breath of God within each of us. Some experiences will be good. Others will fall short. That is because we are material creatures living in limited consciousness, and we will naturally sin and fall short of the fullness of the Divine. This is not an excuse, however, but merely an explanation of what to expect.

As explained in one of my other books, the way that the self transcends the earthly plane—and experiences the eternal planes—is through a raising of vibrations that allows unity to exist with the frequencies of the other world that cannot be perceived by the lower frequencies of this existence here on Earth.

It follows that when we offer the Spirit good experiences, it helps to raise the vibrations within us so that we come closer to becoming the Spirit, that is God, as the essence of goodness. When we fall short of this, we bring down the vibrations within our spirits and create a distance between ourselves and the true reality of God.

When we engage in altruism, we feel good about ourselves. Sometimes, this can be masked as charity or even selfishness parading as altruism, but when we actually enact truly good behavior, kindness, generosity, and love, we feel good about what we have done. There isn't even a need for recognition or acknowledgment of our goodness. The only thing that matters is the act of goodness that we have just committed, and the result is the natural reward of feeling good about it because we have just given God a taste of what is good in life.

When you serve others genuinely, you feel better not just because it is a nice feeling, but because you have stimulated that part of your being which is connected beyond your physical self. You have awakened a higher frequency within you which is literally moving you closer to Heaven. You are awakening the very nature of God's spirit within you. Our calling, then, is to do good so that we may raise our frequencies and elevate ourselves to the higher metaphysical planes where the Spirit within us gets connected to the vastness of God.

God-pull vs Gravitational pull

Think of this as the God-pull. This is opposite to the gravitational pull which is always exerting force on us to pull us in toward the center of the Earth, just as it equally pulls the Earth in its orbit around the sun. Instead of being pulled down, the God-pull is a force that pulls us to something greater than ourselves. There is a longing within us that seeks unity with God. As God is not the ruler of this world, but instead of the Heavenly realm, that yearning does not come from our base, human form, but from the presiding Spirit within each one of us, which is found in our breath and is dedicated to a pull from God.

Imagine, if you will, a kite. It is inevitable that gravity acts upon it. It sits on a store shelf in a box, or in a bundle in a storage closet, or with a tangled-up string in the corner of your garage. It is still a kite. It has color, shape, and design behind how it has been built. But it is not really doing what a kite is meant to do. It is meant to soar higher and higher, and you can see when you fly the kite that the ribbons are swirling, the color is more brilliant, and the swooping and the waving of the kite through the air brings about the kite's real essence.

In the same way, you are a person. You have been designed by the Creator. Creator gave you His own piece of spirit as the breath within you, but if you do not use that breath for goodness, you are just like that kite in the bundled heap in the corner of your garage. The way that you could experience the goodness of the essence of who you are is when you untangle your strings, pursue goodness in the world, spread your arms, and allow the God-pull to elevate you to soaring heights above this world. Up there, you have a new perspective, you have a new life, and you are a fuller version of yourself. That is what it is like when you do good. The next time you feel the pull of a kite string in your hand, you will be reminded of the same God-pull in your life.

Heaven Around the World

If you have been tied to a false idea of Heaven as a fulfillment of earthly pleasures and desires, you may be asking yourself now if Heaven is truly worth it. Some people are not in the habit of doing good, and thus may not feel very comfortable doing the good that is expected of them in this world.

Oftentimes, humans feel the need to have a reward in order to justify behavior they do not want to engage in. Just as a child must eat their vegetables in order to get dessert after the meal, many people ask for a delicious chocolate cake to await them after the arduous task of eating their vegetables. It is only when you grow older that you realize that vegetables were very good for you. It is imperative that you take care of your body and eating vegetables is one way that you can do this. In time, you may even find that you like the taste of certain vegetables and come to look forward to this part of your meals throughout your day.

So, too, as you develop in your spiritual understanding of this life and the next, you will come to realize that the seemingly tiresome tasks are actually of benefit to you.

Think back to the last chapter when we touched on the metaphor of the kite. Of course, kites do not have feelings or desires in the same way humans do, but even for an inanimate object, it is obvious that a kite is more of itself when it is flying high. You, too, have the potential to fly high.

The key difference is, the kite can only go as far as its string will allow it. It is still, at the end of the day, tethered to the earth and dependent on the winds of the world and the will of the one who is flying it in order to stay afloat on the breeze.

If you are able to attain the realization of the heavenly realm, you would transcend the need for this Earth, the weights of existence here, and even the burdens of waiting for the right breeze. Heavenly existence is so far beyond what we can ever hope to know here on Earth.

Jesus speaks in Matthew 11:11 to his followers and tells them that, "Verily I say unto you, Among them that are born of women there hath not risen a greater than John the Baptist: notwithstanding he that is least in the kingdom of Heaven is greater than he."

At the end of the day, even the highest kite is still... just a kite.

Jesus is telling his listeners/followers that John the Baptist—who has a very close proximity to Jesus Himself (they are cousins after all)—is the highest among men. Before we proceed further, let us look at what he is saying. Elsewhere in the 3rd chapter of Matthew's gospel, John the Baptist is described thus:

he that was spoken of by the prophet Esaias, saying, The voice of one crying in the wilderness, Prepare ye the way of the Lord, make his paths straight. And the same John had his raiment of camel's hair, and a leathern girdle about his loins, and his meat was locusts and wild honey.

This person, who Jesus Himself says is the highest among mortal men, is someone who wandered around in the wilderness crying out, whose clothes were made of camel's hair, who had a leather girdle along his loins, and who ate locusts and wild honey.

If we were to stumble on a person like that in today's world, we would likely think of them as being homeless or crazy or, perhaps, needing help. That is who John was.

What made John great was not wealth or riches or connections or comforts or influence. It was his proximity to Christ and, ultimately, his willingness to learn His truth and share that truth with the world. He did so by baptizing many people in Jesus' name, hence the nickname, "John the Baptist."

So, then, what can we learn from this? Is Heaven worth it? Let us think of it this way. The greatest of all humans was John the Baptist who clearly lacked all the earthly pleasures we think of today. Still, it was he who fulfilled his soul with goodness and nearness to the Divine, making it obvious that Heaven would be so much more than that.

Jesus, Himself says that even though John is the greatest of men, he would still be below the lowest person in Heaven. The absolute highest men on Earth cannot even begin to compare themselves with the lowest souls who are in Heaven. This should give us all we need to know that Heaven is a fulfillment, unlike anything we can ever imagine without limited human capacity.

Not only that, but the heavenly realms are eternal. So much of the suffering of this world comes from the fact that everything must reach an end. Our loved ones die, our relationships change, what we value is no longer available to us, and as the saying goes, "all good things must come to an end."

In Heaven, this is not true. That is a promise, then, that the goodness that is known in Heaven is not only beyond the comprehension of goodness known to us here on Earth, but also that it doesn't just last for a brief period of time. Our eternal souls will get to know the joys of Heaven forever. We will carry our good memories, and our cherished experiences with us from now until always. Ultimately, a decision about if Heaven is worth it is a subjective one. That being said, Christ clearly has shared with us the good news that Heaven is worth more than you or I could ever imagine. If you believe in Christ, then Heaven is completely worth it.

Heaven Around the World

The concept of Heaven spans across cultures, religions, and societies each with its own colorful and miraculous visions of what this place may actually be like or, not at all, which will be briefly outlined to understand the various ideas and concepts of Heaven. The idea of Heaven as a place where we go at the end of our lives provides a sense of belonging for us in this infinite universe but offers a knowing that at the end of it all, we already possess the unique design on our very own epitaph without having to plan it. The cultural references to Heaven that exist across religions have some similarities, but also vast differences that tell a story across time and place with unique imagery, concepts, and even characters. Though some of these perspectives describe the realm of Heaven and bring different aspects of culture and society to it, the many questions that arise, for those where the concept of Heaven exists, not only ask what it is but how we can get there and where we are on our path.

Judaism

Let's begin with one of the oldest religions in history, Judaism. While Judaism is known as one of the most ancient traditions and originated among the ancient Hebrews, it is the way of life for modern Jewish people. A surprising concept for those who may not be familiar with this religion is that "as one of the oldest and most influential religions in existence, Judaism might be expected to be the source of our most profound notions of heaven, but it isn't" (*Heaven and Hell*, 2007). This is not a faith based on receiving redemption in an eternal Kingdom, it is one more focused on the here and now. There is very little reference to the concept of Heaven in Judaism; however, this religion does follow strict adherence to rules in culture, society, and life. While the focus and honor is devoted to God, the main tenets of this religion are having "the patriarchs depicted as objects of God's blessing, protection, and providential care. Their response is loyalty and obedience and observance of a cult (i.e., a system of religious beliefs and practices) whose ordinary expression is, vow, and at an altar, stone pillar, or tree" (Pines, 2022). Though followers of Judaism are some of the most traditional people devoting their life to God, the religion of Judaism does not have an emphasis on Heaven or arriving at this place after death.

Islam

Turning to a nearby part of the world and whose religion also reigns across extensive history and society, Islam believes and supports the concept of Heaven. Known as *Janna* in English translation, it refers to the idea of Heaven and eternal life that also has a sub-layer known as *Jahannam*. "Muslims believe in death and eternal life which comes after death. For leading a good life, what actions and qualities are desirable and what impact will be in our hereafter life due to our actions and deeds in this life, we should know about the concept of heaven and hell. Muslims believe on Judgment Day after that

Allah Almighty will decide on the basis of individual deeds where to send in Jannah or Jahannam" (Quran Reading, 2023). The idea that there are levels of Heaven labeled as two distinct places that determine where one goes after death is interesting and certainly sets the stage that one must live a highly moralistic life to reach the highest level of the Islamic eternal afterlife.

Believers of Islam are encouraged to have good deeds in this life because, on judgment day, they will be judged and placed in either of these abodes within Heaven. This is further explained in the Quran itself "See how We have bestowed more on some than on others, but verily the Hereafter is more in rank and gradation and more in excellence" (Quran, 17:21). The concept of Heaven in Islam parallels the glorious and blissful life that the Heavenly Kingdom offers in terms of having abundance, joy, and pleasure that is in alignment with other religions. It "is the description of Paradise, which the righteous are promised, wherein are rivers of water unaltered, rivers of milk the taste of which never changes, rivers of wine delicious to those who drink, and rivers of purified honey, in which they will have all [kinds of] fruits and forgiveness from their Lord" (Quran, 47:15). This glorious place defined within the Quran is only deserving to those who demonstrate good deeds in this life and even then, devotees will still be directed and placed in Heaven according to these two levels. Having a structural Heaven based on the deeds and good will of its followers ensures that those striving to get there and be in the better place of Heaven must indeed be worthy.

Buddhism

The multi-level position of the Heaven of Islam based on noble behavior can be starkly contrasted with the role of Heaven in Buddhism. In Buddhism, the concept of Heaven is referred to as *nirvana*, which is a transcendental, blissful, spiritual state that includes understanding the Eightfold Path as acting, speaking, and living in the right manner and with the right intentions (*Heaven and Hell*, 2007). While Islam believes good deeds will get you to the place of God, the *nirvana* of Buddhism represents the high moral spiritual state within the mind that is the form of Heaven. To reach this state, followers of Buddhism are encouraged to follow The Eightfold Path which teaches a way of being that enables you to free your mind and liberate your life from suffering.

Nirvana is not a physical place as in the Heavens of the Kingdom of God. Buddhism does not believe in God or in a place where you go after you die. The main tenet of this religion focuses on this life and good behavior to receive spiritual merit that is determined by your karma. "In the Buddhist view, karmic results are not considered to be a 'judgment' enforced by a God, Deity, or other supernatural beings that controls the affairs of the Cosmos. Rather, karmic results are considered to be the outcome of a natural process of cause and effect" (Encyclopedia of Buddhism, 2022). This cause and effect will essentially determine your spiritual state which leads you to enlightenment. The Buddhist version of enlightenment is a mental state that is possible to attain in this life and represents the ideal spiritual salvation essentially void of God and Heavenly pursuits but rather is viewed as the heightened individual state as its prime directive.

Hinduism

The many gods of Hinduism are thrown about in our modern world with the spread of yoga and meditation across the globe. Images of gods such as Ganesha, Lakshmi, Kali, and Shiva are just a few of the sculptures that dance across the lounges of yoga studios and wellness boutiques offering spiritual salvation through the eternal sound of "Om". Hinduism is as ancient a religion as it gets with the origins of the Hindu Upanishads with a focus on philosophical inquiry into the nature of the self, centuries ago. The various representations of deities do not equate with the one God, the Creator, but rather individualized symbols each representing areas of your life that can be either supported or destroyed through prayer, focus, and visualization. Hinduism also challenges our notion of reality as being real as determined by the level and power of our ego and leads us to live in an illusion as the basis of our reality.

The Upanishads also acknowledge that "our actions connect us to this world of appearances, which is in fact illusory. What is real is *Brahman*, the ultimate reality that transcends our sensory experiences. Unfortunately, we live in ignorance of *Brahman* and act according to our illusions. This action (*karma*)causes us to participate in the cycle of death and rebirth (*samsara)* from which it's difficult to escape." (Heaven and Hell, 2007) This acute and accurate depiction of Hinduism with the cycle of death and rebirth does not have any connection to the concept of Heaven and in fact perpetuates itself until a high level of self-awareness, and enlightenment, is reached and the state of *Moksha* is attained.

The main premise throughout the Upanishads, the Sanskrit texts still supported in Hinduism today, is that we live in an illusory world. "Hinduism is similar to Buddhism in some ways because salvation—or *moksha*—is reached when the worshiper is freed from the cycle of reincarnation, and his spirit becomes one with infinite consciousness. One becomes free by ridding oneself of bad karma—the effect of evil action or evil intent. This can be done in three different ways: through selfless devotion to and service of a particular god; through understanding the nature of the universe; or by mastering the actions needed to fully appease the gods." (*How to get to Heaven*, 2022). According to the first and second methods, it is through devotion and introspection combined that one can be free from this illusory world and attain the highest state of enlightenment referred to as *Moksha* or *Brahman*. The state of *Moksha* is also referred to as *Brahman*, that is attained when you then have reached the highest state of one's consciousness, "when all longings that are in the heart vanish, then a mortal becomes immortal and attains *Brahman* (infinite consciousness) here." (Quotes from Upanishads,

2022, Katha Upanishad). The Upanishads document many philosophical perspectives and strategies to attain these enlightened states that in essence have no reference to the concept of Heaven most commonly referenced in Christianity.

Christianity

Christianity is the only religion that teaches that there isn't anything one can do to earn or pay their way into Heaven. The only way to get to Heaven is through Jesus Christ and it is through people's faith in Christ as the son of God, they will get to him. Jesus said, "I am the way, and the truth, and the life. No one comes to the Father except through me" (*English Standard Version*, 1971, John 14:6). Jesus Christ died on the cross for the sins of man and was resurrected, just as the spirits of Christians go to Heaven to be in the Kingdom of the Father. For those who give their life to God, as the first promise in Revelations, God will give his Kingdom; "to him that overcometh will I give to eat of the tree of life, which is in the midst of the paradise of God" (*King James Bible*, 2017/1769,). As the remainder of the chapters will focus on what Heaven is and how we may find it, indeed, it is important to clarify that not all religions across the world and throughout history have the same meaning and expression of Heaven in their belief systems. While reading these chapters, this book encourages you to connect with your inner radar and locate that place of Heaven within you that resonates with your soul amid the perplexities of life's challenges and whose answer is simple to your own eternal knowing. Even if some questions arise, the depth of your own inner knowing will guide you in the direction of what you can feel and perceive as your embodied faith and what calls to your mind and heart.

How does One go to Heaven? Are there any Minimum Requirements?

It is a question familiar to many of us. We are curious about what the bare minimum is that we can do and still get into Heaven. If you want to pass on to the next grade, you don't need an A+, you just need, at least, a C average to move on.

To be quite honest, it is rather simple to move from the basic kindergarten level of existence to, at least, the first-grade level of Heaven. Your faith and trust in God through Christ is all that you need and this is available to each one of us.

There are 2 minimum requirements:

1. Existence of a Soul
2. Faith and Trust in Heaven, God, or Christ

We will discuss these 2 requirements. But first, let us discuss what components constitute each one of us that is unseen.

God's Spirit with-in

Each person is endowed with the divine spark of life from the Creator God that provides and sustains life in a physical material body. This divine spark residing inside of you is your Spirit. The fragment of God Himself, which is bestowed to each person in all glory of uniqueness and delight, can be referred to as spirit.

Then the LORD God formed a man from the dust of the ground and breathed into his nostrils the breath of life, and the man became a living being - Genesis 2:7

The spirit is God's indwelling presence within this spark and is always connected to Him. The spirit is known by many names across spiritual teachings, including and not limited to....The Higher Self, the Indwelling Spirit, the Over-soul, the Ka, God Fragment, the Thought Adjuster, and many others. While these terms are expansive and represent different elements of our perceptions and ways of understanding God, the main idea is that the spirit seeks its expression in the lives of its indwelling hosts, or in other words, us humans. When this expression of spirit is manifested, it creates the connection of God within the non-physical element of every human who embraces their spirit, thereby supporting the notion that we are all "One."

"You are made in the image of God" (Genesis 1:26-27).

The Spirit of God within is pure and clean as God and just as perfect and pristine as it was when God gifted it to us at our birth. This bestowed divine spirit indwells in you, patiently waiting until you are ready to acknowledge and start to work together. One of the main teachings of Christ on Earth was to awaken humans to this divine presence within. The more you explore your Inner Kingdom, the more God is revealed to you

That which is eternal is required

The physical self is, however, easy to be polluted. Our thoughts and actions and the way that we neglect our physical bodies take a toll over time and we are left with increasingly marred and imperfect bodies. To be clear, this is not a statement on people who may have different physical abilities. No one is "less than" because of needing a wheelchair any more than someone would be considered imperfect because they need glasses. No, this is specifically about defiling the body with impurities that, regardless of physical capabilities, will eventually happen to all human bodies. While the physical body can be so degraded, used up, and will ultimately experience death, the Spirit does not and cannot be polluted by our thoughts and actions. In fact, the Spirit, because it is of God, is just as pure and clean as God and just as perfect and pristine as it was when God gifted it to us at our birth.

Upon the death of the mortal physical body, your identity, and your personality will end here unless there is something that is beyond the material realm which can carry your experiences, your successes and failures, all your good and bad experiences which gives you a character and unique personality. Only if there is such a thing that can exist after material demise, one can exist eternally.

I declare to you, brothers and sisters, that flesh and blood cannot inherit the kingdom of God, nor does the perishable inherit the imperishable.
- 1 Corinthians 15:50

So if the spirit cannot carry your essence forward into eternal life, then there should be something else that is needed to carry your essence, your character, and your personality after death. This new essence is called Soul. This is God's gift for eternal life.

Birth of a Soul

At about the age of four to five years old, the material mind starts to become mature enough to make moral choices. If you have children, or if you remember your early years, you know that this is about the time when enough learning has taken place that a child is beginning to listen, question, explore, and make decisions that can impact others greatly. Too much before five, and the child largely doesn't know any better.

At around age five, there is the beginning of the new entity that will continue to grow with the child as it matures and ages into adolescence and young adulthood. This new thing comes about by being birthed of the material mind and the indwelling spirit that makes way for a new entity that is neither material nor non-material. It is, instead a semi-material matter known as the soul.

The mother of this new entity is the material mind and the Father of this new entity is the non-material spirit. The semi-material nature that we popularly call the soul. Many books refer to this as Morontia as well.

This semi-material construct carries your self, personality, and identity. It contains the temporal identity familiar to us during our limited time here on earth as well as the pre-personal spirit, which existed before our physical bodies came into being and which has the potential to carry on after we experience death sleep here on earth.

Because we have the semi-material soul, we have the blending of the human (the personality of the material mind) and the Divine (the identity of the spirit) which gives the capacity for the self to experience life either as human or divine. The choice as to how it goes about this liminal work is up to us. The soul gives us the potential as the intermediary between the physical and the nonphysical, between material human and non-material God, but only through our own intentional choices do we amplify the part of the soul that leans towards the Divine and away from our base, limited, and ultimately temporary physical selves. The soul is another selfless gift of the Divine. It comes from God and gives us the opportunity to become God-like while still living in our human bodies. Now that we understand the relationship of the soul to the other parts of the self, we must examine the purpose and choices of the soul.

Just as each person is unique here on Earth (even identical twins have their own bodies and minds), a soul is the unique identifier of the person in Heaven. The soul is that part of you that is eternal. You would not be able to experience the eternal Heaven through your earthly body. It is not meant to last beyond the time apportioned to it on Earth, and thus it would be incapable of hosting your true self throughout all of eternity. Only a soul can do that, which is why it is essential to have faith so that the self has a vessel through which it could experience the eternal goodness of Heaven. 1 John 2:17 tells us the words of the apostle John who wrote, "And the world is passing away along with its desires, but whoever does the will of God abides forever." Only in choosing to have faith in God will you have the opportunity to abide forever.

All your experiences are stored in your soul and become part of the soul's DNA. Every thought, word, and deed has an impression. Everything is an energetic vibration and gets recorded in the soul-DNA and becomes a part of your identity. When God or Christ see you, they see your soul as your identity. They do not see the physical appearance that you might identify yourself as. Transitory physical identification is an illusion in some ways, yet these combined components of your soul signature develop throughout your life as your soul's DNA evolves into your unique energetic expression.

Once you have a soul, you are an eternal being with a unique signature in all of creation. God and the angels will identify you with your soul signature. Your name and physical body no longer carry meaning. The truth is they never did. Those were only placeholders for your true self.

Jesus says, "For this is the will of My Father, that everyone who beholds the Son and believes in Him will have eternal life, and I Myself will raise him up on the last day."

For children less than 5yrs who are not ready for Soul yet, what hope do they have? The rules for young children are relaxed. Please refer to Book-2 of this series Welcome to Heaven, wherein we will discuss Families, Relationships, Children, Marriage, Sex, Job, Food, etc..in Heaven.

Faith is the ticket to Heaven

In Matthew 17:20, Jesus speaks and tells his Disciples, "If ye have faith as a grain of mustard seed, ye shall say unto this mountain, remove hence to yonder place; and it shall remove, and nothing shall be impossible unto you."

Moving mountains seems impossible in this world, but let us be reminded that Heaven is not of this world. The kind of faith that can move a mountain is the kind of faith that can get us into Heaven.

In Ephesians 2:8, Paul echoes the teachings of Christ when he writes to the church in Ephesus and tells them, "For by grace are ye saved through faith; and that not of yourselves: it is the gift of God."

At first glance, this may seem at odds with our purpose, as previously discussed, to do good in this world so that the breath of God within us may recognize the goodness in the experiences that are tied to our earthly bodies. Part of that goodness, though, is the recognition of the Spirit within us that is of God. All goodness is centrally tied to that, and the acknowledgment of that reality is what we know as faith.

Born of the Spirit

It is the willingness to be God/Christ-like, the person is "Born of the Spirit", and they become worthy of the first level of Heaven. It is a way to graduate from the kindergarten of planet Earth and to transcend into the first-grade level of the celestial state.

It is said in the Bible; "Truly, truly, I say to you, unless one is born again he cannot see the kingdom of God" (NIV, John 3:7).

Born again soul is a child of the universe. The soul has eternal life.

The Christian community acknowledges this choice and this birth through the ritual of baptism. Remember that John the Baptist was seen as the highest among men, and part of that was through the actions taken as a baptizer. A baptizing ritual is an act that is symbolic of having a soul.

A baptism is historically something that the church has done to try and prevent people from going to hell. Many different Christian churches practice infant baptism because they believe that if the baby is not baptized and if they happen to die, they won't be able to get into heaven. Again, this is close to the right understanding, but not quite. The baptism is not in and of itself the salvific act. The immersion in the baptismal is only the outward symbol of the internal confession of faith that the heart goes through. Remember, it is not just words that can gain someone access to heaven. In the same way, empty acts without true conversion will also not lead someone to heaven.

Your responsibility on Earth is to try and attain the highest level of Heaven available to you. To be clear, your responsibility is different from your purpose. Your purpose in school is to get educated. Your responsibility is to do your homework, read the assignments, and study for the exams. The better you fulfill your responsibilities, the more whole and total your purpose will feel to you.

Book of Life

When a person chooses to have faith and is willing to trust God, that person gets "Born of the Spirit", and they become worthy of the first level of Heaven. It is a way to graduate from the kindergarten of planet Earth and to transcend into the first-grade level of the celestial state. The souls' identity is written in the book of life. The soul exists forever.

Our responsibility on Earth is to try and attain the highest level of Heaven available to us. To be clear, your responsibility is different from your purpose. Your purpose in school is to get educated. Your responsibility is to do your homework, read the assignments, and study for the exams. The better you fulfill your responsibilities, the more whole and total your purpose will feel to you.

Understanding Earth as a Kindergarten School

Every person reading this is obviously a person who has found themselves on Earth. That means that you have the Spirit of God dwelling within your breath and working within you. There is a release of so many of this world's distinctions that remind us of that truth.

Just like in kindergarten, you are taught that no one person is better than anyone else. No matter a person's age, gender, race, or abilities, every person is the same in the eyes of God. Like the Sunday School song says, "Red and yellow, black and white, they are precious in his sight, Jesus loves the little children of the world." Although it is a seemingly cheesy kid's song, it would be good for us to consider it as a reminder of the simple lessons of childhood when we approach the vastness of God's true self and the potential we have for revelation within God.

Because you are on Earth, you are the same as every other person who is here. It doesn't matter how much money you have, where you live, or what experiences you have gone through in life. You are the same as the person breathing next to you.

Other planets were also a part of God's creation of the Universe, but they are not the same as Earth. God has specially designed planets like Earth that are called seed planets. They serve as training grounds for younger potential souls. These seed planets are there to help a person with a spirit, or breath-of-life, to experience life and grow closer to God.

Earth happens to be the one that you and I occupy, and while we can take solace in the fact that no one of us is better than any other, we are all in a difficult situation together here on this particular seed planet.

Kindergarten is your Foundation

Clearly, there are difficulties on this planet. It is not the easiest to be on, but that does not mean that it is not good to be here. Earth is literally the place where our spiritual foundation needs to be built. Before it is even possible to step further into Heaven, we need to have a firm foundation.

Just as all buildings, whether a house, a castle, or a skyscraper, need a solid foundation, so, too, a firm foundation is needed for an individual's faith and trust in God to be able to soar into the heights of the heavenly realms. This time here on Earth is not just special; it is vital to a person's spiritual potential. With the right foundation, there are practically limitless heights for the soul to climb onto to experience the heavenly realms.

Time on Earth is thus necessary for the future of the soul. One's faith and trust in God and a desire to be like God will ultimately determine the strength of the foundation.

Spiral Ladder of Evolution

To this point, we have used the overarching metaphor of Earth as a kindergarten, and we have also looked at our purpose with the help of a metaphor of a kite. Now, it may be helpful to look at the difficulties of Earth through the lens of a spiral ladder.

Imagine a spiral ladder that extends from Earth to all levels of Heaven. The lowest rung from where the ladder starts is what we have referred to as kindergarten and is where we find ourselves on Earth.

The ladder is a spiral-like construct because there is no strict delineation of consciousness or dimensions. It is not as though it is a trip to another horizontal plane. Rather, it is an elevation through a connected way of ascension that results in a higher place just over our own understanding. Because it is a ladder to the

Heavens, it extends almost infinitely and the rungs become narrower as the height increases.

The narrow stairs symbolize the great difficulties in the higher levels. Only through extreme care and attention can we navigate through the difficulties of the higher levels. It takes more and more work to ascend higher and higher, but you can see that the stairs keep going, thus it must be possible to continue the climb. There is not really an end to the growth and learning in God's creation.

Once a person has developed proper and transformative faith in God through Christ, there has been a demonstration of the minimum requirements to attain admittance to Heaven. If you have faith and trust in God or Christ and desire to be God/Christ-like, you have a ticket to Heaven.

Lucifer Rebellion and Planet Earth's Unique Opportunities

Earth is in a unique situation and has been for the past many thousands of years. This is a direct result of the Lucifer Rebellion. You may be familiar with the story of the fallen angel, but if you are not well-versed in religious texts, we will summarize briefly to say that the War started in Heaven and spilled over into Earth. If you would like additional information, there are a couple of references in the *Bible* to the Lucifer Rebellion found in Revelation 12:7-10, Isaiah 14:12-15, Jude 1:6, and in a few other scattered places. These references are sketchy at best and do not paint the whole picture.

Essentially, Lucifer, who was a high heavenly being, rejected God's plan for creation. Lucifer did not want to be under God's authority, he wanted to become God and wanted his own creation. He was able to sell his creation concept to 1/3 of the Heavenly angels and waged a great war that caused him to be cast out of Heaven. At that point, he and his trusted person Satan and took up dominion over Earth.

If you are interested in this fascinating subject, I do have a book named "Lucifer Rebellion. Christ vs Satan – The Final Battle for Earth has Begun". This is one of my passions and best works. This will most likely become a major movie at some point. Will leave a link at the end of this book if you are interested.

Due to the effects of the Lucifer Rebellion, Earth has become an extremely tough school for young souls looking to experience life, choose faith, engage in goodness, and achieve even the most basic levels of Heaven, let alone any that require higher vibrations. Among all of the seed planets, Earth has the most extreme duality of good and evil.

God is aware of this and applauds each and every one of you just for being present here on this battlefield known as Earth. It is so difficult here that our existence requires God's constant supervision every day and every night. God has given us free will, and although He chooses to watch over us, He does not choose to intervene. This makes it so difficult for us, but it is a part of the creation God has given us.

The only way God does intervene is if it is part of a higher purpose that achieves a heavenly goal we cannot understand, or if we ask for a change in experience through our time of direct prayer to Christ.

As we mentioned earlier, it is simple to move between kindergarten and first grade, or from Earth to the heavenly realms. Just because something is simple, however, doesn't mean it is easy. The simple thing is to understand, but the more complicated thing is to carry out appropriate actions based on that understanding.

God does not use a magic wand to remove all sorrows

We have seen Earth as a very hard school, but, thankfully, God, Christ, and all the cosmic hierarchy are aware of this reality. This is why we receive so much grace and mercy as compared to other parts of creation. We are given every benefit from Paradise God to give us the chance to graduate or, at least, to escalate our growth.

Of course, God does not use a magic wand to transform our lives. That would not be granting us the agency of free will and the choice that lies therein. It is still possible, however, that God might use a few people to bring light to the many. However, the general process is that we all, you and I, learn from our mistakes and grow into better beings, who are closer to choosing the faith in God required to leave this Earth.

In God's eyes, we are all a lot like a bunch of kindergarten-going children who are trying to have wonderful experiences. However, there is an older bully who is lost in the classroom and who is constantly trying to get us to jump in mud puddles, spill paint on purpose, kick the teacher, and refuse to take a nap during quiet time. Other classrooms do not have to deal with these kinds of distractions that are born of menacing intentions. The bully thinks he will win if we refuse to learn anything and stay stuck in kindergarten forever, making bad choices that harm us or those around us.

God, however, is like a loving teacher or parent who is guiding us consistently and with great patience toward the right decisions that will yield goodness in the classroom, a helpful learning environment, and the chance to learn.

The choice is ultimately our own, however. We can choose to listen to the bully and act out in ways that distract our classmates from learning. If we choose this way, we, too, will not learn and, we will instead suffer the consequences of our actions. We can, however, choose to listen to the teacher, even if the bully is being loud in the back of the class, to be able to understand something that is enough for us to graduate to first grade.

The teacher, God, cannot simply wave a magic wand and give us knowledge. God does not just transform the creature of gross animal nature into a perfected spirit through mysterious acts of magic. If God's desire is for every human to be perfect, He would have already created us perfect. The experience for a perfect being is almost zero; the learning is zero; the potential for growth is zero. Having said this, God did create perfect Angels for purposes that we do not understand. Our choice is to listen to God so that we may, of our own volition, transform our animal natures and become closer to the eternal beings we are all trying to become.

Skipping Levels and moving to Higher levels of Heaven

Graduation from kindergarten means you have taken the steps up from the bottom rung and have managed to find yourself on a higher platform into the first-grade level of Heaven. To be clear, though, we are all on Earth together, experiencing the same kindergarten, and we will not all graduate to the same first-grade experience of Heaven. Depending on a person's personal growth on Earth, they will end up in various different levels of Heaven.

While it is extremely difficult, it is possible to skip a few grades and attain an even higher level of Heaven. Think of it as going from kindergarten to high school. Every once in a while, you hear of a child prodigy, but, for most people, the jump is too high. It is not easy to navigate the steps once they become narrow. The spiritual tests of faith and trust become intense as one progresses in the understanding of God and creation. After a person's mortal death (also called death-sleep), the person's soul and spirit go through a clearly defined resurrection process. This resurrection process will attune you to the corresponding body (or vehicle of expression) that is relevant to your next phase of evolution. Your soul vibration will match the level of Heaven you are ready for. This can be a bit confusing or too much to take in for a novice, but it is sufficient to understand that every bit of effort you put on this Earth plane for your Soul growth is not wasted. God's creation is infinite, your soul has a purpose in His creation.

The way that one achieves this is through service to God and determination to know and be more like God. In this way, a person can give rise to a different soul experience, higher vibrations, and more elevated graduation into a much higher level of Heaven. In Matthew 6:19-21, Jesus tells his listeners:

Do not lay up for yourselves treasures on earth, where moth and rust destroy and where thieves break in and steal, but lay up for yourselves treasures in Heaven, where neither moth nor rust destroys and where thieves do not break in and steal.

With this reminder, we can be reassured that our good karma can help us transcend the meaninglessness of this world's so-called treasures, and result in achieving higher heavenly levels.

Heaven, after all, is our true and eternal home. Good karma and good deeds, and service, will determine how high you climb the staircase. The higher you are, the more elevated your light quotient will be, which will ultimately be what determine how far you can go into Heaven.

Just as we have discussed the requirements to graduate from Earth to Heaven, there are other requirements for the different levels of Heaven. Mostly, this has to do with a soul's vibrational frequencies. To live in a high vibrational frequency of Heaven, your soul must be a vibrational match.

Sadly, as we are only mortal beings, the requirements to the highest levels of Heaven are yet unknown to us, but we have been made aware that the idea of the elevated vibrational frequencies is, at least, one of the prerequisites for the other levels. As you progress, God will reveal the other heavenly goals to your soul, and you will again have the choice of whether or not you want to work to attain those levels.

If you choose to continue climbing the staircase, your body will also transform to accommodate the level of growth that you have achieved. Just as your earthly body is relevant to your time on Earth, your self will move through different heavenly bodies, only if you are able to continue your climb up the higher levels of the true soul.

WHAT IS THE GRADUATION PROCESS FROM KINDERGARTEN TO FIRST GRADE?

When a person graduates from one level of schooling and proceeds to the next, there is often a ceremony that commemorates the occasion. Most often we think of high school or college graduations, but there are graduation ceremonies for many children who transition from kindergarten to first grade as well.

But, why is this such an important phenomenon? Isn't it just enough to be done with school and to have completed your education? Why is the graduation ceremony such a monumental occasion? The ceremony is about much more than sheer nostalgia or an honoring of age-old traditions.

There is meaning in the transition from one level to another. It is important to recognize and pay attention to it. So much of our life can pass by without our being even aware of how we have changed or grown in the process. It is rather easy to move from one thing to another without a ritual to acknowledge the change that is occurring in our lives.

For education, it is important because it is when the actual diploma becomes conferred onto a person. In front of peers, family, and friends, there is a sense of recognition of the hard work and dedication offered to the person who has gone through the steps to become educated and finish high school or get a university degree.

It is, indeed, very different from your graduation from planet Earth, but there is still an important ritual experience that a person's self must go through.

Graduation from a school may require tests and an adequate grade point average. However, graduation from Earth, as we have established, is about faith and trust in God. We are not asked to provide proof of our faith or good deeds on our graduation day in order to proceed from this temporal realm to the eternal ones. As long as we have faith and trust in God, we are assured of our place in the graduation ceremony.

We have learned that a person's Soul gets born when a person is about 5yrs old. The soul is a semi-material substance and does not perish along with the mortal body. We have also learned that when that faith is established, (most often recognized by a different ritual ceremony known as baptism), the person is granted 'eternal life' status. The soul, henceforth, carries your identity and will be the vessel that carries your memories, emotions, deeds, and actions permanently from this life into the eternal existence that begins from beyond this life.

How, though, do we move from our physical body that is also occupied by our soul to a purely soul-self? This is the graduation process.

For what does it profit a man to gain the whole world and forfeit his soul?" (Mark 8:35-36)

What exactly happens when your mortal frame dies?

The physical body cannot exist in the eternal heavenly realms. It does not make sense to expect a body that is subject to the ravages of time, decay, and a general breakdown of itself, to be able to exist for eternity. If a good body can only last 100 years here on Earth, it has no hope of carrying itself through to Heaven.

So will it be with the resurrection of the dead. The body that is sown is perishable, it is raised imperishable – 1 Corinthians 15:42

The body that a person who is graduating from Earth to Heaven will have is not going to be much like the body that is being held today. It won't look like a young version of yourself or be an expression of your body in its prime. That isn't how it works. The body will be totally different, but it also won't matter because the body won't carry with it all the value we place on our bodies today.

This is important because people who are differently-abled physically or who have had trauma to their bodies will not carry that with them to the eternal realms. The body that you will have, should you be able to contain a soul. This body in heaven will be a semi-transparent body that is Soul-like. This is also called a soul-body or Morontia body (according to some books on this subject). The combination of these parts of the body into one unified semi-transparent body is known as resurrection.

It is important to note that in Heaven you will be Soul like; while on earth our identity is skin deep, your identity in Heaven is your soul. Your beauty, your identity in heaven is your soul.

The Transition from the Physical Body to a Soul body form – The Resurrection

The resurrection, that a person with a soul will have, is not about returning to Earth, however. There is no longer a need for this kindergarten experience. There is no opportunity to repeat a grade. Instead, you are resurrected to this new body and a new way of experiencing your being. This body will be more suitable for the experience you are about to have in Heaven. Just as you need a submarine to take you to the bottom of the ocean instead of a car, a Soul body (or Morontia body) will be the vessel that is most fitting for the heavenly travels that lay ahead of you.

For the perishable must clothe itself with the imperishable, and the mortal with immortality. When the perishable has been clothed with the imperishable, and the mortal with immortality, then the saying that is written will come true: Death has been swallowed up in victory. 1 Corinthians 15:53-54

The process of transition between these two forms is not immediate. Once a person graduates from earthly kindergarten to the first level in Heaven, that soul needs time to acclimatize to this new level, having come from the earthly level below.

There is more than just a bodily transition taking place during this time, too. During this grace period, which can last a few months, the soul is given permission to visit earthy loved ones. It is a form of closure, which is also important for the graduation ritual. In being able to conclude the time on Earth, the soul is freer to travel faithfully into the future realm.

Many people in our world today have shared experiences of having felt the presence of their loved ones for a short time after their physical death. You may know someone who has claimed to have seen the person walking in their familiar home, walking a route they used to walk, or even sleeping in their old bed. These sightings are not of the physical body but are an experience of this in-between state. After some time, again no more than just a few months, the soul then decides that it is ready to move on to continue to pursue the next lap of the journey.

There is a lot to the resurrection process. The Spirit, Soul, Identity, and Soul-body are involved. This is an intricate but precise process. Many Heavenly beings are involved in your resurrection process. The detailed resurrection process is discussed in Book 2 of this series "Heaven". This is absolutely worth it to know what a resurrection process entails. I highly recommend it. Will leave a link at the end of this book if you are interested.

Jesus Christ's Resurrection Process

The resurrection process that a soul-embodied mortal person goes through is similar to what Christ has gone through with some differences. Christ resurrected in the physical body with His soul-body wrapped around His physical construct which is converted to light. If Christ had a fully physical body externally all disciples and others would have easily recognized Him. Yet no one recognized Him until after He spoke or made Himself known. The resurrection process of Christ is quite fascinating. It requires an in-depth understanding of the Heaven and resurrection process itself. Very few have this depth of spiritual knowledge to tackle this extraordinary event. I do have an entire book that talks about Christ's resurrection process, basically the 36 hrs. between death and resurrection. If you are interested, the book is titled – "What Happened on Easter Saturday. 36hrs mystery between death and resurrection.". Will leave a link at the end of this book..

What happens to non-believers, people of no faith in God?

Your soul and your spirit ensure that your identity remains intact at all times as you progress through the ascension journey across the different levels of Heaven. In the time scheme of the universe, we are children walking across a bridge between the material and the spiritual, the finite and the infinite. The mere fact that we are children, however, does not mean that there is an excuse for us not coming to God. Unfortunately, if someone does not take the time during their life to fulfill their purpose, come to know Christ, and develop real faith and trust in God, there is no way that they will have a resurrection experience after the death sleep.

The reality is that not everyone will come to have faith and trust in God during their time on Earth. It is not a guarantee of this life, and many people will lose out on the opportunity to gain eternal life for themselves.

In spite of all opportunities provided on the material level of existence, if a person chooses consciously not to believe in Heaven and does not exercise faith in God or Christ, the soul will not have the opportunity to move to the next level of experience. The soul identity will perish along with the mortal frame. This makes God extremely sad.

For the living know that they will die, but the dead know nothing, and they have no more reward, for the memory of them is forgotten. Their love and their hate and their envy have already perished, and forever they have no more share in all that is done under the sun. Ecclesiastes 9:5-6

Those souls who have consciously rejected God and have no faith, these souls will be lost forever after death sleep. What a waste of this precious gift of life this will be. There are many on earth at this time without faith and trust in God (billions of humans), sadly they will not experience the goodness and eternal life of heaven. Your job and my job is to reach out to those who are looking to know God and the meaning of life itself and leave the rest to God.

In many ways, this is sad, of course. We don't like to think of people we may know having potentially missed the chance of having a soul and thus gaining Heaven. This is why it is so important for us to use our time wisely on Earth. Everyone is given the same opportunity to come into a deeper knowledge of Christ, and if that is not realized, then the consequences of that are real for everyone who fails to utilize the gift of time given to them.

Christ is, however, exceedingly merciful. Of all beings, Christ uniquely knows how difficult life on Earth is. With that in mind and knowing that Christ was such a pivotal part of quelling the Lucifer Rebellion in Heaven which resulted in the evil one's realm being established on Earth, it is important to realize how much grace and divine mercy Christ is consistently pouring out on everyone in this realm, even the most undeserving among us.

Hope abounds in Jesus' very nature and there is a desire to have as many people enter Heaven as possible. Some false religious teachings will perpetuate the idea that there are a limited number of people who are saved or who can experience the next levels of Heaven. This is not true and it does not come from God. Christ is wanting to have each person gain a soul and eternal-life status through faith and achieve Heaven. If that were not true, Christ would not have come to give us such powerful teachings and show us the way to Heaven.

There are many whose faith flickers, what will happen to them?

Please do not let this alarm you. It does not mean that occasional sin, mistakes, or falling short of the ultimate glory of God, will keep you out of Heaven. All people can go to Heaven in spite of their imperfections. The forgiveness that comes from God is immeasurable. If this is not the case, there would probably not be anyone in Heaven other than Christ and it would be a lonely place. By truly seeking forgiveness and showing a contrite heart, we can join the multitudes of souls who have come before us and gone on to Glory in Paradise.

Life on Earth is extremely harsh, it is not easy for a person to exercise faith in God or Christ while things are not going well. Most people fall into this category. God and Christ are very aware of this and have great compassion for all of us earthlings.

In fact, this is the very basis for Christ's first coming. It made the way for human graduation to first grade. Without Christ's time on Earth, we never would have the avenue forward that is available to us now. It is, after all, only through faith in Christ that we get the chance to attain Heaven, and so Christ makes that opportunity available to us all.

It is not always black or white, there are various shades of grey. People's faith flickers. Human experience in this limited consciousness is not an easy task. Even angels prostrate what humans are going through each and every day.

If a person is not able to acquire faith during this Kindergarten school, the person will not graduate to Heaven after death-sleep. However, depending upon the Soul's potential to evolve or strengthen his/her faith, the soul is granted "Potential to Survive" status. Many souls on earth live in darkness due to their own making or due to circumstances not under their control. Also the environment the soul is in plays a big part in soul development. Taking into account all of these considerations, the Soul is granted "Potential to Survive" status. These souls go into a deep slumber state. They reside in this state until a time known as the "End of age divine dispensation", which happens only once in a millennium or so.

DEATH SLEEP – DEEP SLUMBER UNTIL HARVEST

These souls who have the "Surviving Potential" go into a deep sleep or slumber upon mortal death of the physical body. So the Soul and identity are preserved at this time. Since these souls are not ready for graduation yet, but have the potential to graduate.

This slumber exists until there is a divine event where certain important decisions are made. These divine events happen about once in a millennium. During this incredible event, great divine grace and mercy are showered. Another name for God is Mercy and Grace. Christ's First Coming and Second Coming events are such events.

Christ First Coming Event – Harvest

During Christ's first coming, He was able to save a lot of these slumbered souls from Abraham's bosom as Holy Bible calls this. (Luke 16:22)

Christ Second Coming Event – Harvest

During the second coming event also Christ is expected to save a whole lot of slumbering souls. Bible calls this Rapture where the dead will rise and be saved. The second coming, which will be at a time, and in a matter yet unknown to us, is expected to grant even more divine mercy and additional chances for those who do not yet have exercised faith. With great divine mercy and many opportunities over long lifespans here on Earth, a good harvest is expected.

Heaven is precise, the souls are individually accounted for. People who have the potential are in billions. I will choose not to give specific numbers. The numbers keep changing all the time. Extra time granted to us is an act of divine mercy.

The Various Levels of Heaven

The information included in the next two chapters is fairly advanced. It is a part of this book because it gives a complete picture of the different levels of Heaven as it relates to our location on the planet Earth.

It would only be natural if the previous chapters led to further questions about the ongoing development of the soul, the structure of Heaven and Earth, and what the other worlds outside of this one are made up of.

Depending on one's spiritual maturity, some concepts might be new. Please do not get too caught up in the difficulties and complexities of this chapter. If it feels like this is too advanced for you, feel free to skip it.

Heaven is a location, not a mind concept

Most of us have some concept of Heaven, even if it has been characteristically one formed by movies like *What Dreams May Come or The Lovely Bones,* or thinking it involves meeting as in the movie *Bruce Almighty.* Just as a movie requires a set direction and props, Heaven may just as well be similarly designed, but by one of the best designers, set directors, and make-up artists combined into One and by God Himself. It is created by "the One", the Father who brings all things into being. The many levels of Heaven are as deliberately designed as any stage or movie set and include an intentional structure and order to creation that has existed since the dawn of time. Most certainly when we come to understand that our very soul, spirit, and identity are equally quite remarkable, then it comes as no surprise that Heaven too is just as real and astounding a place as the rest of all creation. In this chapter, we will explore the basic physical structure of Heaven and the various levels this Kingdom possesses.

While we can dream and imagine the white puffy clouds as being pillows that tuck us into our angel feather beds at night, and eternal sunshine exists as our backdrop as we float through in the expansive blue sky each day, it's actually not like that! Rather, Heaven is an actual location and not a mind concept. As taught by Jesus, he said, "I go to prepare a place for you" (*New International Version*, 1973, John 14:2). This place, Heaven, as told by Jesus, is prepared and planned. This intentionality of Heaven can set us at ease. We tend to put God in a box and try to explain with our limited conscious understanding what things are all about when in reality, God determines all, and we are only human after all. Imagine and allow for the incredible graces of our Holy Father to plan and have a dwelling place for us and know this to be true. When we can do this, the concept of Heaven becomes easily understandable and grasped as a relatable place that is waiting for us. The Father is loving and He has prepared for you a multitude of worlds on which you will continue to accumulate experience. It is simply impossible to gather all of the experiences of your soul's destiny in just one world, and only the initial one at that. When you have the path of the whole of creation laid down before you, with limitless experiences and boundless worlds, there are eternal structures you will see that will amaze you along your journey.

The Structure of Heaven

While you may be a beginner or have many years of growing and expanding your spiritual foundations on your relationship journey with God the Father, you may already know that Heaven is a place with multiple locations. We have established that it is not one single place but that the number of locations is varied and even infinite. For some, this may be common knowledge, whereas, for others, it may be a new concept. Regardless, bringing you the reader to this point of awareness and comprehension is key for this part of the book and for the remainder of the chapters as we will begin to traverse the physical structures of Heaven as well as our layers of consciousness to get there. Be sure to go slow and take time to explore, understand, and integrate the following concepts that support ideas relating to the structure of Heaven, especially if some of these ideas may be new to you.

We can classify the structure of reality and worlds as categorized as layers into 3 broad categories that range from the material world being the most-dense to non-material as the least dense. Then there is Paradise where God, the deity resides.

1. Material worlds (physical worlds like Earth)

2. Semi-Material worlds (transition worlds, also called Soul or Morontia worlds)

3. Non-material worlds (Spirit Worlds)

4. Paradise (God's abode, beyond time and space)

The structure, makeup, and complexity of worlds increase as one moves from the lower to the higher dimensional levels not in physical complexity, but in their frequency. Imagine that each level corresponds with a dimension. The less-dense we are in the material world, the higher the frequency in the less-dense dimension. And, the frequencies of higher dimensions are more complex than the ones below. Let me explain this further. If we were to place living beings in the most-dense material plane, it is easy to comprehend that the chemical composition and complexity of the level above is higher than the level below yet appears and is more physically dense. Higher levels or dimensions require less food or sustenance than a lower-level living being would consume but are more complex in frequency. Overall, it is therefore safe to assume that food or sustenance requirements will reduce as body-form frequencies increase.

Think of it in relation to the concept of vapor that rises without having form or density. The higher you go, the higher the senses become and less sustenance is required. At some point, experiences beyond the five senses will start to open. This can lead to the understanding that the abilities that people have in the higher Heavens are more complex than what we are accustomed to and may be represented through advanced telepathy or having other super-sensory skills or powers that equate with being generally common for that level or dimension. Forget the internet, imagine how fast messages could arrive if they were simply sent and received on a mental signal that didn't require opening up your email and reading it, let alone finding the "on" switch. The three worlds are broken down individually and outlined below and will clarify the different levels of existence to which our human body, soul, and spirit can experience after our earthly death sleep.

The Three Worlds of Space and Time

Material world (Physical worlds like Earth)

The material world is right outside your doorstep. We are fully aware of this earthly plane that can be felt by the ground that we walk upon, the seasons that change in our geographical locations, and the tides of the water that rise and fall with each phase of the moon. Each part of our Earth and its sphere is made up of certain chemical elements, for example, periodic table elements that all have certain vibrational frequencies that are not only found within our bodies but also the planet as a whole. For those who are familiar with the Shuman resonance, it acknowledges that "each lightning burst creates electromagnetic waves that begin to circle around Earth, captured between Earth's surface and a boundary about 60 miles up. Some of the waves—if they have just the right wavelength—combine, increasing in strength, to create a repeating atmospheric heartbeat known as Schumann resonance" (Wilson, 2013). These incredible electromagnetic waves are present around us and keep us in the earth's container, grounded in physicality and energetic impulses that make up and define the material world. The

Earth, as we know it, also contains physical and dense beings—we humans—that require food and sustenance for our bodies. It is the food that we consume that fuels our own living energy and keeps our cellular structure, blood flow, and heartbeat alive, all maintained within the unique properties of this material dimension.

Semi-material worlds (Transition worlds also called soul or Morontial worlds)

While Earth is a planet with a density we are certainly familiar with where we can walk, drive, and even fly in an airplane as part of our experience, what are the semi-material or transition worlds? *Morontia* is a term that refers to the vast level suspended between the material and the non-material (spiritual planes). There are many sub-levels within this realm. Each *Morontia* world is characteristically more refined, complex, and considerably less dense than the one below it. While knowledge or even awareness of these worlds is not very common or well-known to most people, they are documented in the Bible.

One of Jesus' own disciples wrote about an 'enduring substance' of Heaven that can lead one to contemplate the existence of the *morontial* worlds, as it is written in Hebrews; "For ye had compassion of me in my bonds, and took joyfully the spoiling of your goods, knowing in yourselves that ye have in heaven a better and an enduring substance." (*King James Bible*, 2017/1769, Hebrews 10:34). As you rise in these semi-material worlds, they become less dense and, according to this biblical reference, existence has a more timeless frequency that may be best measured and described as immortality. Once we begin to transcend the earthly realm, vibrational frequencies increase, and the spaces contain beings who are less dense and whose bodies need less food and sustenance for survival.

While it may be strange to think of beings other than humans who live in other dimensions and these angelic or other beings of reference are new to you, these beings living here have a body form technically called *Soul Body*. When Christ was resurrected, Christ's body was a *Soul Body* form. This is semi-material. If it was not, doubting Thomas would not have been able to touch the wounds of Jesus Christ whose biblical story demonstrates the importance of believing and having faith; "then he said to Thomas, 'Put your finger here, and see my hands; and put out your hand, and place it in my side. Do not disbelieve but believe.' Thomas answered him, 'My Lord and my God!' Jesus said to him, 'Have you believed because you have seen me? Blessed are those who have not seen and yet have believed'" (*New International Version*, 1973,). Not only does this story represent the power of faith during the time of Jesus' resurrection, but the form of Jesus' body was a *Soul Body*. If His body was fully spirit, He would not have a form to be recognized by the apostles during His resurrection. Many did not recognize Him at first glance, unless He revealed Himself, meaning He did not have a pure physical body. When we begin to imagine the spaces beyond our physical and material world, and the impermanence of our life and our own physical body, it clarifies how incredible our own human body is and the fact that a *Soul Body* and other creatures exist is entirely fathomable. Perhaps it is when we acknowledge the spiritual world and complete transcendence that many begin to scratch their heads and wonder if spiritual ascension is feasible. This semi-material world may introduce some notions of *Soul Body* and impermanence, but it is the spirit worlds that take us to yet a higher frequency even more astounding.

Non-material Worlds (Spirit worlds)

The spirit worlds might be easier to imagine if you have spent time watching science fiction movies of mythical realms and creatures that walk on other planets. While you witness and experience the visuals of these places through colorfully filmed productions, the spiritual world, distinct from the physical world, can be perceived just as incredible. But true depictions of the spiritual world may not be entirely possible due to subjective realities and our lack of ability to perceive them. I will do my best here to describe these spaces of the spiritual world that may not elude all of us. According to the best of my knowledge and experience, there are numerous spirit worlds. As we can best imagine they are different from the material world grounded in the earth. The spirit worlds have energy wavelengths and celestial bodies that require food and substance yet at a much lesser frequency. The spirit is 100% light and therefore there is no substance to the body form. There is no need for food or sustenance for the celestial beings that are 100% light because the spirit is self-generating. It is possible that many beings who are from spirit worlds came to Earth as planetary teachers and are walking among us.

If you can imagine the spirit as light, then it is possible to comprehend that the vibrations of a spirit being is very high, meaning that their frequency operates not on the dense emotions of fear, hate, or sorrow as an example, but contains more love, joy, and gratitude. Aside from the amount of information that we can find on the internet these days, presently and historically we have seen pictures of these celestial beings with halos around their heads, like those of Christ, and maybe even floating above in the air. I believe this represents a self-generating glow of Spirit. This representation of divinity or beings of divine stature is celestial beings who live in the spirit worlds that surround us and exist on different dimensions. The spirit world is a level that is one dimension lower than Paradise, the abode of the Holy God, the deity.

Paradise – God's abode

The best possible attempt to describe and define God's abode and utilize the most appropriate English word possible would be *Paradise*. This place isn't referring to the five-star hotel situated on the turquoise oceanfront property of a tropical island that we may dream about but, if you set your imagination on a place that is uniquely unfathomable to our limited consciousness, you might just be able to comprehend it. Why is the word "Paradise" appropriate to refer to Heaven? When understanding the origin of the word Paradise from early English, French, and Latin, it has interestingly enough been directly translated as 'The Garden of Eden' (Etymonline, 2022). This makes this choice of the word quite appropriate, it appears, as it relates to the book of Genesis as one of the first Books in the Bible. The Garden of Eden "is the story of the heavens and the Earth when they were made, in the day the Lord God made the Earth and the heavens" *(New International Version*, 1973, Genesis 2:4-6). Paradise is used frequently throughout the Bible including in the book of Luke when it says, "and Jesus said unto him. Verily I say unto thee, Today shalt thou be with me in paradise" (*New International Version*, 1973,). Paradise is the dwelling place of the Trinity—God the Father, God the Eternal Son, and God the Infinite Spirit— and conjures many ideal qualities to define the Heavenly Kingdom.

Paradise is the indwelling place of all beings and is where God himself resides in the Kingdom of all eternity. When a person dies, the soul and, as we addressed in earlier chapters, the spirit detaches and goes to Paradise to be in the presence of God. If we can suspend the limitations of our human consciousness momentarily, we may be able to grasp the infinite concept of this resurrected place referred to as Paradise. We can identify it as a place that has no time and exists in one eternal moment. Since everything created has movement, for example, the planets, stars, sun, and galaxies that are in constant motion and so in tune with the expansiveness of the universe and unequivocal harmony, there is another end of the spectrum. It is possible to imagine that no time or space can exist either. Can you imagine it? Can you resonate with both perspectives of the duality of the existence within our universe created by God? Is it possible to comprehend or exist in absolute movement and utter stillness while being in a timeless place where God exists in all realms with an eternal presence? Many do believe this is possible.

I have created the image below representing the three worlds of time and space. Material worlds have physical body forms. Semi-material heavenly worlds have Semi-material body forms also known as Soul body forms. The spirit resides in spirit worlds. Then there is Paradise which is beyond the time-space continuum.

There is a graduation process that happens as we progress in our evolution. We will talk about the graduation process between different forms shortly.

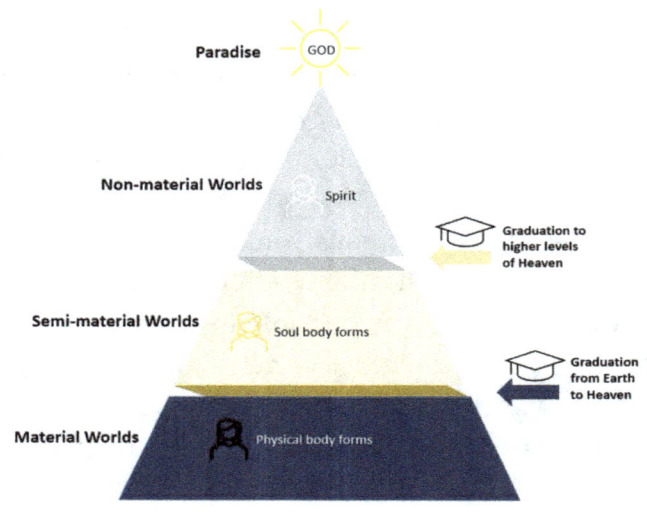

Is there Graduation and Post-Graduation in Heavenly School?

So that you have a complete picture, I have decided to give an overview of the next level of graduation, which can be considered Graduation, post-graduation, and beyond.

God is infinite in all aspects, and so is His creation. There are infinite experiences for a soul or spirit to experience just as there are many levels to Heavenly experiences. This may be difficult for our human minds to contemplate. Putting God's creation in a box and stating this is all there is, is similar to stating there is only a grain of sand on a beach.

When I was young, studying Bible and growing in Christ, I was under the impression that there is only a big and large room in Heaven where everyone goes after death. All fall down and worship God forever. This kind of life seemed a boring and also appeared to me that God was some kind of dictator. Thankfully I grew out of that not notion as my conscious learning experience began to take shape.

On Earth, when a person does his/her 10th grade and high school, the students feel they know a lot about life and everything there is. When the same person completes graduation and post-graduation, they get a feeling that there is a lot to learn and they know very little. When the same person completes a doctorate and or multiple doctorates (or Ph.D's) they will then realize that what they know is minuscule or nothing, their knowledge is just a drop in the ocean.

This is the same with Heavenly knowledge.' God's creation is infinite and growth is also infinite. There is one big advantage that Humans have that Angels are jealous of. We will discuss that in the next chapter.

I will share some fundamental concepts from my understanding, so please do not get too caught up in the difficulties and complexities of higher consciousness levels of Heaven.

In Matthew's gospel, Jesus tells us in chapter 7, verses 13-14: Enter through the narrow gate. For wide is the gate and broad is the road that leads to destruction, and many enter through it. But small is the gate and narrow the road that leads to life, and only a few find it.

The road that we travel becomes narrower as we continue to progress on the journey. That does not end just because we have managed to gain a soul and eternal-life status and advance beyond Earth into the heavenly realms. As one progresses in spiritual maturity, the road becomes narrow, spiritual tests become harder. Have you ever seen a superhero who had an easy ride to power and fame?

Jesus' words are cautionary as we leave this place. They are meant to be a part of a firm foundation upon which the soul can build itself as it advances through the levels of Heaven. The spirit, just because it advances through Earth, will still have opportunities ahead of it that could be detrimental to progress. The broad road and the wide gate that can lead to destruction are not just found here on Earth but are constant companions along the journey that our souls are on.

This is because we will always have free will. Under any circumstances, Angels do not interfere with the free action of the human will. They do not invite the sanctity of the human mind or manipulate the will of mortals. This is because you have everything that you need without the angel's help. The spirit of God is within you, and the opportunity for faith and trust in God is always before you. For the angels to manipulate the individual would cheat the system of God's design.

To be certain, neither the angels nor any other order of the universe has the power or authority to curtail or abate the prerogatives of human selection. Even in this realm, which is a part of Lucifer's domain, even Satan cannot corrupt the mind. All that is offered is the wide road ahead of us.

Because of this, it is not possible to cheat or to buy your way into Heaven. It is in the very fabric of creation itself that a being has this tier time on Earth to prove their worthiness and advance further to become associated with the eternal realms. If that is not achieved, that being simply will not survive the frequencies of that level of existence. In this experience, the person passes through every level of consciousness of their own volition. Because of this, the person knows better how to approach the more complex structures of the advanced levels of Heaven.

For our purposes of understanding, which is within the bounds of our limited human intellect, we can broadly categorize the structure of the Heavens as follows:

First, there are the material worlds. We currently exist in one right now. The Earth is not the only physical world, but it is the one we are familiar with. There are others scattered throughout the various planes of the universe, but all of the material worlds lead to the semi-material worlds.

Semi-Material worlds are also known as transitional worlds. As we mentioned before, Morontia is an in-between state between the physical and the spiritual. It is when the spirit and soul occupy a form that is vastly different from the earthly physical body, but it is not the highest, purest level of vibration that presents as pure light to be seen in the Spirit worlds.

Spirit worlds are non-material, and the 'bodies'—for lack of a better word and for the purposes of making sense in our limited imagination—are at their highest frequencies and present themselves as pure light. Of course, pure light does not really become contained in a body in the way we think of bodies here on Earth, but this should give you an idea of the way that the vessel for the soul progresses in the upper levels.

The structure and complexities of these worlds keep increasing as we move from the lower to higher dimensional levels. In fact, at this point in time, and even with Jesus' words of guidance, we cannot know all of the complexities of the higher levels and, probably, never will... until we are able to be there ourselves.

We do know, however, that the material requirements are reduced, and the vibrational frequencies are heightened as the person progresses to the higher worlds. Food, sustenance, sleep, and other basic needs to maintain a body slowly fade away as the person transitions from a physical body into one of pure light.

Semi-Material Worlds

We have previously used the image of the spiral ladder to help us conceptualize the distance and the way between the various levels of Heaven. To continue that metaphor, let's look at the next few rungs of the ladder beyond the bottom rung.

Just as a butterfly metamorphoses from a caterpillar, the ascendant mortal emerges from the earthly tabernacle of the body into the soul-body form upon resurrection. The resurrection mortal is made up of the semi-transparent form which is a combination of the soul, spirit, and personality. The world that this body inhabits is also a combination of these materials.

When we are resurrected from the death sleep, we are not reconstituted as creatures of flesh and blood. Rather, we are resurrected as soul-like bodies that are semi-transparent or semi-material. This is the same body that Christ inhabited after His resurrection. This is a fascinating process.

It is important to know that this is not the final state of the body. If you did not know any better, you might think that this new body, because it is so different from the one that you had previously inhabited, is the final form of your soul self. That is not the case. This is more of a transitional body. Just as a person in middle school is much more grown and developed than a baby, they are not yet a full-grown adult and have so much growing up left to do.

The seme-material body is fused with the soul fused which is semi-material also. You are your Soul-like in this body form. The spirit, however, is still separate and is not fused with the soul.

During life in the soul-body form, the soul must make an everlasting decision to become one with the spirit within. It is a big decision and just like the way that the angels do not interfere with the will of the person on earth, they do not interfere here either.

God is already a part of us at this point and the decision ahead is for our soul-body form to choose to become a part of God. Here, we make the decision to do God's will, to eventually become perfect as our Paradise Father is perfect. This melding with God ensures that we will enjoy eternal life as one with God.

While this sounds glorious, it requires our walking over the narrow path that eventually leads to a dissolving individual path, and the person, as we think of them, ceasing to exist so that God may exist more fully... with our individual being incorporated as part of God, the Paradise Father's eternity.

Spirit Worlds

When a soul has matured enough and is pure enough, it eventually becomes ready to undergo a fusion with the spirit. Up until this point, the soul and spirit occupy the same body but are two distinct parts of the self. Oftentimes, we conflate the two in our romantic or religious literature, but they are not at all the same.

As Jesus told us through the gospel of Matthew, we know that the road becomes even more narrow as the soul continues to ascend. There may be additional proof or tests required of us that we are not aware of, but conceptually, there is not a commonly held belief that it would be very different from what we experience on Earth.

Ultimately, the idea is that, just like being on planet Earth, spiritual development is going to be an opportunity available to all and gained through acceptance, trust, and deeper levels of faith. God has shown time and again that beings are not asked to be tested or to endure any difficulty. God's grace and mercy prevail here on Earth, and we know that this is a challenging seed planet to exist on. If our pathway forward is rooted in God's mercy and revealed through our decision to have a deeper faith and trust in God, then it is assumed that advancing beyond the higher levels will be an even more profound way for the soul to come to develop spiritual proximity with the Paradise Father.

When that transition toward a fusion between the soul and the spirit forms does happen, we do know some specifics about what characteristics will be a part of that being.

The spirit level being is one of pure spirit. What pure spirit means is something beyond what we can fully comprehend, but we can catch a glimpse through our knowledge of our own small piece of spirit within us, known as our breath, and, of course, through the teachings of Christ.

With enough spiritual maturity and purity, the Soul earns the right to merge with the indwelling spirit. The soul, and spirit are fused in this transition and they become one. When this fusion happens, the person becomes a pure spirit. A pure spirit takes on an entirely different form from what we have considered previously. This form does not have the same outlines or contours of the physical body or even any Morontial forms.

When this transformation happens, there is a graduation ceremony similar to the one that occurs during the transition between Earth and the first level of Heaven. It is not the same ceremony itself, but it is the same concept that the ritual is necessary for the transformation to occur.

This fusion of soul body and spirit is your graduation (like a 4-year college degree). You become One with God. There is no separate body or soul or spirit, it is all spirit that contains all the experiences of the soul since Kindergarten. Your spirit henceforth becomes a storehouse of all future experiences in this spirit realm.

Even the word 'form' might be a bit of a misnomer as the being becomes 100% light with no physical form at all. The physical frequencies that can elevate or decline throughout time on Earth are consistently high. The vibrations are so high because they are so light. If you were to look at light waves, you can see that they are much higher than sound waves or microwaves. Light is at such a high-level vibration that the purest form of the spirit becomes befitting for this plane of existence.

At this level, it is not only up to the individual to invite the change. Because it includes the Divine, there is a need for there to be a heavenly representative who can be the arbiter of this transformation. It follows, then, that Christ is the gatekeeper for this level of conversion. Only through Christ's invitation can one hope to move between the semi-material world of the soul body and the non-material world of the spirit form.

We know this because of what is found in John's gospel. Jesus tells his disciples in John 14:6, "I am the way, the truth and, the life. No one comes to the Father except through me." This is a reference to the Paradise Father and to this specific conversion between the soul-body into the pure light of the spirit form.

Without Jesus' explicit invitation, a soul body can never hope to attain a full spirit form. Only through Christ, a soul can become a spirit and be able to visit Paradise (Holy God's abode). This is what Christ meant by words – "I am the way, the truth, and the life"

Many humans have manipulated the words of Christ to fit their own misguided agendas. More often than not, it is for religious institutions that are aimed at perpetuating their own self-interest instead of preaching the true words of Christ. While the basic idea of faith in God through Christ is paramount to moving beyond this world, the truth is much greater than what makes sense here on Earth.

Christ is the way, and not just a knowledge of who God is. More importantly, Christ is the only one who can invite mortals into the spiritual realms that are elevated beyond the basic levels of Heaven.

When the being is invited into a metamorphosis that yields the most elevated level of Heaven of pure light and highest vibration frequencies, the being enters Paradise which is the ultimate abode of God, the deity.

Paradise

The paradise trinity is beyond mortal or even angelic comprehension. God is the deity and is not within our capacity to understand. In fact, it would be ignorant and foolish to even begin to attempt to decode the deity of all existence.

Paradise is beyond space and time and, as such, it is fitting for it to be the realm of God, but also past our limits of knowledge. Even though we cannot know it, there are still scriptures that point the way toward its existence so that, at the very least, we might know that it is true and it lies beyond the end of our spiritual journeys.

Deuteronomy 14:1 reads, "Each person is precious because God created each person in love and with his divine spark, and for this reason, God has given them His law." Because

God gives each of us the divine spark, there is a part of us that ultimately knows the way.

Other biblical evidence can be found in reference to Christ being seated at the right hand of the Father. Hebrews 1:3 reads, "When he had cleansed us from our sins, he sat down in the place of honor at the right hand of the majestic God in Heaven." This is just one of many scriptural attestations to the locality of Christ in Paradise alongside God in Heaven. This is also spoken of in Hebrews 12:2, 1 Peter 3:22, and Acts 7:55-56. This is not meant to be a metaphorical idea of Jesus being close to God, the Father. This is a literal sharing of Christ's position at the right hand of the Paradise Father in the ultimate realm of spirit.

Only when a being has completed their journey through spirit levels, and only on the condition that they become invited by Christ can they move through a graduation ceremony and into this final realm. They, too, can be at the right hand of the Father. These beings are known as Paradise Finaltiers, due to them reaching the ultimate tier and finally entering Paradise.

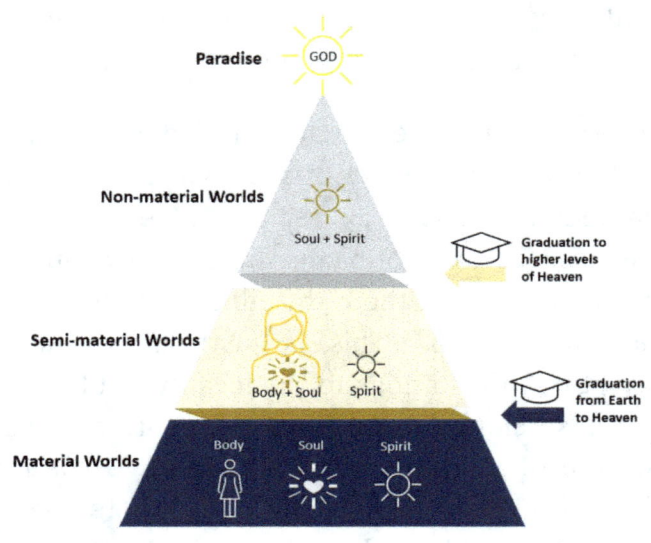

Questions and Answers

We started with a few questions, let's answer those based on what we have learned so far.

1. Isn't Heaven just a mind concept? What is the proof of its existence? Is there biblical evidence?

- Christ calls it His "Fathers house" (John 14:2)

- It is called "Paradise" (2 Corinthians 12:4, Rev 2:7)

- The "Kingdom of Heaven" (Mathew 25:1, James 2:5)

- The "Everlasting Kingdom" (2 Peter 1:11)

- A "better country", "a heavenly country" (Hebrew 11:14-16 NKJV)

- The third heaven (2 Corinthians 12:2 ESV)

- Christ said – My kingdom is not of this World (John 18:36)

- "Heaven and the highest heaven" (or "heaven and the heaven of heavens") (1 Kings 8:27, Nehemiah 9:6, Psalm 115:16)

- Paul says - They have in heaven a better and more enduring substance (Philippians 3:20-21)

- "Then I looked and heard the voice of many angels, numbering thousands upon thousands, and ten thousand times ten thousand (Revelation 5:11-13)

We can make the following deductions:

- Heaven exists, Heaven is not a mind concept, it is a location, a dwelling place

- Heaven is a "better country" or good place to look forward to

- It exists forever (everlasting kingdom)

- It is worth our effort (eternal inheritance)

- There are 3 or more levels (third heaven)

- Heaven is GODs house (Father's house)

- There are many mansions or many levels in heaven (In my father's house there are many mansions)

- Heaven of Heaven (indicating levels)

- Kingdom of Christ (My Kingdom) – Every kingdom must have subjects, organizations, order, structure

- There are an infinite number of Angels in Heaven – (thousands upon thousands, and ten thousand times ten thousand)

2. Why do I even bother about Heaven? What is in it for me?

From the above Holy Bible references, we can deduce that pursuing Heaven is a worthy idea. Heaven is an eternal kingdom and your eternal inheritance. If you choose to survive after death with your personality and experiences, Heaven is the way forward.

3. What are the minimum requirements to go to Heaven or the ticket booth to Heaven?

The minimum requirement for Heaven is the presence of a Soul and your conscious choice to have Faith in God, Trust in God, and a desire to become Christ-like or God-like.

4. What is Spirit?

Every living thing that has breath has God's own spirit in them. This is the breath of life that functions in you and me. This spirit within gives us life. You and I have God's own spirit within us. Hence we are made in the image of God. You and I have a direct connection with God.

5. What is a Soul?

Children about the age of 4 to 5 old, the material mind starts to develop the will and make conscious decisions and moral choices. At this age, there is the beginning of the new entity that will continue to grow with the child as it matures and ages into adolescence and young adulthood. This new thing comes about by being birthed of the material mind and the in-dwelling spirit that makes way for a new entity that is neither material nor non-material. It is, instead a semi-material matter known as the soul.

The mother of this new entity is the material mind and the Father of this new entity is the non-material spirit. The semi-material nature that we popularly call the soul. The soul is both material and non-material at the same time. This semi-material construct is the storehouse of all your experiences, both good and bad, successes and failures. This gives you a personality and Identity.

6. What are the minimum requirements to go to Heaven?

There are 2 minimum requirements:

1. Existence of a Soul

2. Faith and Trust in Heaven, God, or Christ and a desire to be God or Christ-like

7. What does being born of spirit mean?

It is the consciousness willingness for a person to have faith and trust in God and a desire to be God/Christ-like, the person is "Born of the Spirit", and they become worthy of Heaven. The born-again soul becomes a child of the universe. This soul is eternal. It is the only way to graduate from the kindergarten of planet Earth and into the celestial state.

It is said in the Bible; "Truly, truly, I say to you, unless one is born again he cannot see the kingdom of God" (*New International Version*, 1973, John 3:7).

The Christian community acknowledges this choice and this birth through the ritual of baptism. The baptism is not in and of itself the salvific act. The immersion in the baptismal is only the outward symbol of the internal confession of faith that the heart goes through. Remember, it is not just words that can gain someone access to heaven. In the same way, empty acts without true conversion will also not lead someone to heaven.

8. What are the main constituents of humans in the material world other than the physical body?

Our bodies are generally made of three main constituents – Physical body (material), Spirit with-in (non-material), and Soul (semi-material)

9. Why life on Earth is our kindergarten school?

We have seen in the previous pages that planet Earth is a training ground for new and young souls. It is here where a soul establishes a foundation. A firm foundation is needed for the next phase of the eternal journey. This foundation is your kindergarten (as I call it) school. With no foundation, structures cannot be sturdy.

10. Is there different levels to heaven? If so, how many?

According to the Holy Bible, there are at least three levels or categories of Heaven.

11. What is the general structure of Heaven?

Other than the material words that we live in, the structure of Heaven is classified broadly into 3categories:

- Semi-material worlds (first levels of Heaven, Soul body forms)
- Non-material worlds (higher levels of Heaven, spirit realms)
- Paradise (Abode of God the deity, beyond all space and time)

12. Does time and space exist in Heaven, if so how is it different from Earth?

We have seen that Heaven is a location and has multiple levels. Every location is subject to the time and space continuum. Levels of Heaven are subject to the time and space continuum. Time and space are very different than what we understand in the material world. In some ancient scriptures of a religion, it is said that 1000 years of earth time is equivalent to one day of Heaven (the highest levels of heaven). There is some truth to this.

From what I understand, one day in the semi-material level of heaven is equivalent to three days of Earth time. This is the reason why Christ's resurrection took 3 days (not 1 or 2 days)

Paradise, Holy God's abode is beyond all space and time. It is one eternal moment. It is beyond space and time. There is no GPS to take a person to Paradise. Kind of difficult to comprehend with our limited conscious awareness. A person cannot go to Paradise unless invited by God through Christ alone.

13. What body will you have in heaven?

When you and I go to the first levels of Heaven, our bodies will be semi-material as well. This type of body is popularly called the Soul body or

Morontia body. This is the same body that Christ had after the resurrection. This is a common body form. The soul will fuse with this body form, thereby becoming soul-body-form. You will be soul-like in this body. Your body will glow with the light that your soul carries. Unlike Earth where your beauty is skin-deep, it cannot be hidden in the soul-body. You will shine and glow that displays your soul experiences. All your experiences are stored in your Soul. The Soul gives you personality and temporal identity. You are your Soul Like.

When you graduate to the Spirit realms, your body form will be pure light with no substance to the form. You are then a fusion of soul and spirit into One. You will have no form or can take any form you desire that fits the purpose. All your experiences are stored in your spirit. The Spirit will become your permanent identity.

14. Where will you go when you die (death-sleep)?

Upon mortal death, if a person has a Soul and consciously exercises Faith and Trust in Heaven, God, or Christ, the soul has the "Surviving Potential". If one's faith is strong enough, then the Soul will be resurrected in Soul-body form in Heaven.

If one's faith is not as strong, but flickers, then the person is deemed as a "Potential Survivor". Upon the death of the mortal frame, the soul is protected and goes into deep sleep or slumber until a time of divine dispensation. The divine dispensation happens approx once in a millennium.

If a person consciously chooses not to exercise Faith or Trust in God, then the soul does not have the capacity to survive after death sleep. The soul will perish along with the body. This makes God and Christ extremely sad.

15. What happens to young children when they die those who do not yet have souls developed?

The rules for young Children are relaxed, this also depends on where the parents are on Earth or in Heaven. The topic of Families, Relationships, Marriage, Sex, Job, Food..etc is discussed in the forthcoming Book-2 of this book series Welcome to Heaven.

16. What happens to all our life experiences on Earth including successes, failures, shortcomings, and illnesses?

Once a Soul is born, it becomes a storehouse for all of your experiences, good, bad, ugly, successes, failures...etc. You are the sum of your experiences. However, some experiences are dead weight and do not serve a purpose for your further growth. This dead weight is like chaff. The chaff is separated from the wheat. This dead weight is your illnesses, your emotional or mental baggage. All these get dropped when you get to Heaven. You will just be your Soul-like. Your experiences give you a unique personality and identity. Your beauty is your Soul-like, it is not skin deep anymore.

However, it is important to note that God does not remove all issues that are less than perfect from your soul. There are lessons that you and I have to learn to evolve. These are like black grains in our analogy of wheat and chaff. These are not removed. It is our responsibility to learn and transform these.

17. Why life on Earth is so difficult? Why is God/Christ not waving a magic wand and resolving all problems?

Duality exists in the extreme sense on planet Earth. This has to do with Lucifer Rebellion. The War in Heaven between God/Christ vs

Lucifer/Satan. This war came to Earth. Lucifer/Satan exercised their dominion over this blue orb. This topic is deep and too complex, almost impossible for most humans to believe. Reality is much more difficult than Scifi. It is my passionate one. My purpose is tied to this unseen war. If you like to know more about Lucifer Rebellion and War in Heaven, check out my book – Christ vs Satan – Final Battle for Earth Has Begun"

18. Does God have a plan and a purpose for you and me and the planet? If so what is it?

God and Christ have plans for each of us individually and collectively. The more one evolves, your puzzle piece will become revealed. However, I should also mention that all plans are changeable and are designed only with your acceptance. This acceptance usually happens on an unconscious level. We might not become aware of the plan until we are evolved enough. These contracts (as I call them) are designed to be activated at an opportune time that depends on many factors including the person's growth and collective Human consciousness

19. Are there relationships and families in Heaven? Are there marriages in Heaven? What

about love and sex? What work do I do all day? What do I eat? Do I have a home? Can I visit heaven while living in a physical body?

Glad you asked these basic questions (smile). If you are curious like me asking tons of questions and wanting to know everything about Heaven, this book might be for you. Please check out the forthcoming book-2 of this series "Welcome to Heaven – Your Relationships, Your Family, Your Sex, Your Job".

The Advantages of Being on Earth's School

Some of the greatest inventions and developments in the history of humanity have come about from people who have experienced extreme hardship. People who have lost parents at an early age are often more likely to thrive and catapult themselves into amazing positions later in life. Maybe they feel that they have nothing to lose. Maybe they feel that they have already lost so much that they wonder why not go for seemingly unattainable goals. What is most likely is that these people have been so honed by the difficult experiences in their early life that they are able to weather any storm that they may be forced to reckon with as they get older.

Think of how people train for marathons or build strength in their bodies. Marathon trainers have to endure long-distance runs that break down the limits of their bodies before they can build up new thresholds of capability. Bodybuilders also have to push their muscles to the brink of failure in order for them to become stronger and be able to grow in meaningful ways.

It is part of the natural world that real growth is not easy to come by. If we are lucky and well-adjusted, we might turn out to be successful or able to learn quickly or have bodies that are easy to train. None of that compares to the ability of a person who has been through the fire and has been tested and trained and has come out on the other side stronger and fiercer and smarter and more capable than how they went in.

All of this is to say that, at the end of the day, we are suffering. It is not a secret, though not many people admit readily how terrible life on Earth can truly be for our mortal selves. Earth is popularly known as the Planet of Sorrows among the heavenly realms. This is due to Lucifer and Satan's Rebellion. As discussed earlier the War in Heaven came to planet Earth. I have detailed this in my book, Lucifer Rebellion. Christ vs Satan-Final Battle for Earth has Begun (link at the end of this book). My purpose on this little blue orb has to do with this Rebellion, just like many who may read these pages.

Other rungs on the ladder look down and take pity on the existence that we have to go through here. Some beings that start a life elsewhere aren't even aware of how bad it can be until they achieve the first level of Heaven and then learn that there is such a thing as the Planet of Sorrows.

Many people believe this is unfortunate. It certainly does make it hard for us to graduate from this life, at least compared to other potential life forms that can facilitate spiritual advancement with relative ease. Our difficulties stem from the root of darkness that has infected this world due to the Lucifer Rebellion, which has already been discussed. This is a sad fact of existence for us, and there is nothing that we can do to take away the reality of the hardships that we face.

That being said, because we are constantly being forced to reckon with such evil forces even in our daily existence, we also have a wildly high amount of potential than other life forms. Yes, this is a hard life and a difficult kindergarten to graduate out of, but for those who are able to train themselves, there is an incredibly high potential for greatness that is not as readily available to occupants elsewhere.

Yes, there is a darkness that lingers, but there is also a great light. At the end of the day, you get what you are looking for. If you are focused on the gloom and the darkness around the world, then those shadows will ultimately consume you. Many of us have probably come across these people. Maybe they appear depressed, maybe they have lost hope, or maybe they are just a person who seems to always have negative things happening in their lives. Whatever the reason, some people are drawn toward darkness. In allowing themselves to be drawn to that chaos, they are opening themselves up to the effects of that chaos in their lives.

The difficulty is that once you allow the darkness to suck you in, it becomes extremely difficult to get out. The shadows are all around you, and it is much easier to continue to stare into the darkness because your eyes have already adjusted to it. There is, however, always the light.

Just as people who look for darkness are able to find it quickly and easily, so, too, are those who look for the light in this world. By "light," we are referring to Christ, God, and the Angels. There are also some of these people that we might have encountered in our lives. Relentlessly positive and cheerful people can make us suspicious at times. We must ask the critical question of where their cheerfulness comes from.

If it is absent of knowledge or faith in Christ, then the cheerfulness is simply a mask and the person is likely looking away into the darkness of the pit. If a person is always positive, and that positivity is centered on the light that they find in Christ, then their good cheer and happiness are a byproduct of being transformed by a relationship with God, which has resulted in a more fulfilled spirit and higher levels of frequencies for their soul to enjoy.

The fact of the matter is that light is easier to shine and easier to see in darkness. That is what we have as an opportunity before us on Earth that other seed planets do not have at their disposal.

There is a parable that comes from the Philippines about a Queen who had two daughters who were both equally qualified to take over the crown after she passed away. Wanting to make sure the Queen leaves the country with the best possible ruler; she decides that she will offer a test to her daughters.

She brings them both to the great hall and her voice echoes around the huge empty cavernous space. She gives both of them 10 gold coins and asks them to use that money to fill the space. The first daughter goes to the market and does everything she can to buy cheap things that take up a lot of space. She uses her coins quickly and is able to buy massive amounts of what is essentially garbage. She hauls the garbage into the space and is able to fill the space without any money to spare but with every inch covered in trash.

The second daughter takes a single gold coin and goes to buy a candle from the market. When the first daughter is done, the second daughter patiently removes all the trash from the great hall and sets the candle in the middle of the great room. She lights it and the light of the candle fills the whole room.

Her mother smiles and lifts up her hand. This child has nine gold coins still left and has used her understanding and wisdom to bring about a much better and more fulfilling wholeness to the room that was needing to be filled.

The truth is that our planet is filled with garbage. And many people think that they are filling the emptiness in themselves and on this planet with cheap treasures. There is, however, another way, and we have the opportunity to be like the wise daughter who uses light to drive out the darkness and to fill the room in a way that brings beauty and goodness.

The light is always there, and it is up to us to determine how best to see it, how to share it, and how to let it fill the great rooms... not just in our hearts, but in the entire expanse of the world that we are a part of. It is not easy and not everyone thinks of it. In fact, most people look around and see only darkness, or if they do recognize that they are witnessing themselves to darkness, they do not always understand that the way to be properly filled is not through massive amounts of trash.

It takes a certain kind of intelligence, cleverness, and, sometimes, the right guide who can show you the way toward the light, which is always available to you. We know that guide is to be Christ and the teachings to be preserved in holy scripture. While this is an extremely difficult kindergarten class to graduate from, it is an opportunity for us to move forward through the most difficult training ground that exists among the seed planets. Think of it as the Harvard Business School of seed planets, because we have the opportunity to emerge as the best beings in the universe if we go through the rigorous and demanding educational system provided to us here on Earth.

There are so many metaphors throughout scripture of there being a light in the darkness that is available to us here on Earth. In Psalms 115, we read, "Thy word is a lamp for my feet, a light on my path." This stresses that light is not only available to us but is also the way out of the darkness if we would only take the necessary steps. In John 1:5, we read the assessment of Christ that says, "The light shines in the darkness, and the darkness has not overcome it." No matter how bad the Lucifer Rebellion was, no matter how strongly Satan has dominion over our planet, it is still no match for the light that comes to us through Christ.

Other scriptures as well help to bolster this understanding—with constant reinforcement of Christ as the light of the world—that our job is to bring Christ's light to the world and to bring glory to our Father in Heaven. That light is for all people, even for those shining in the darkness. Any cursory understanding of the *Holy Bible* will immediately illuminate this constant theme throughout the text.

Even the basic Sunday School children's song is meant to evoke this truth in our spiritual lives, "this little light of mine, I'm going to let it shine..." One of the first things you are taught is to *seek the light*. The more you focus on the light, the better equipped you are to be able to make the choice to have faith and trust in Christ which will offer you the next steps toward graduation from this level.

Most Superheroes have a dark past

If you think about it, most of the heroes in our history are people who have symbolically been a light shining through great darkness. The trials and tribulations of this world are opportunities in disguise, presented to us by God to show how worthy we are of not just the first level of Heaven, but even the higher levels as well.

Some of the most notable examples of people who outshone their dark times include Mother Theresa, Martin Luther King Jr., and Abraham Lincoln. Each one was faced with the scourge of death and destruction wrought upon this planet by the Evil One. Each one of these eminent people, who—it should be noted—were all very close followers of God/Christ, were able to shine out and serve as an example of goodness not just for those in their immediate circles, but for the whole world... and stretching beyond their time into our own.

Yes, while the chaos and darkness of this world may threaten to overwhelm you, and while it does make it difficult to see the truth clearly at times, it is also a chance for our light to shine so brightly that it helps our spiritual journey go even further and deeper than it could on any another seed planet.

Let's consider that one of the more popular genres of pop culture today is superheroes. It is not a surprise nor is it a coincidence that these stories resonate with the human experience/condition so much that entire movie franchises are built, and thrive, around these characters. These characters are vastly different from one another. Some have many powers, others barely have more than a good aim and lots of courage.

No matter what the case is, each superhero has a backstory or a reason why they became the person they became. Nearly every single character has a difficult journey to get to where they end up. Batman lost his parents at a young age. Captain America wasn't good enough as a boy, but became superhuman and then was frozen for decades while all his loved ones died. The Hulk couldn't control his powers which led to personal isolation and loneliness.

All of these characters have amazing potential because they have gone through dark and chaotic times. Without the chaos, in fact, none of them would have become the superheroes that they needed to be.

Superman (my favorite superhero) is a figure that has many Christ-like allusions in the stories, comics, and movies that focus on him as the central character. Superman is not born as Clark Kent. He is from another planet and is sent to Earth when Krypton explodes. He not only loses his parents but also his entire home planet.

Similarly, Christ came to us from a different place that was not this world. Christ's kingdom was not another planet, but another celestial realm altogether. Still, both Christ and Superman were not from this Earth originally but came here to try and do good for people who were not always grateful and who were constantly fighting with one another.

This is not to endorse Superman or any superhero. This analogy is being shared to provoke the thought that these stories are so popular not because people enjoy the flash and pizzaz of superheroes, but because there is a part of each of us that recognizes the potential for greatness within each one of us, the feeling of loneliness, and the potential to shine out in bleak darkness.

This can only be done if the person embraces their powers or the Spirit of God that is within them. If Superman chose, he could have been Clark Kent the entire time. Only through willingly choosing to be Superman was he able to perform superhuman feats of strength and rescue so many people. So, too, each one of us can choose to remain humble. Life can be simple and doesn't have to present any challenges. But we have the potential to rise up above that and flourish if we unlock the faith and trust in God that is within us. Superman is not of this world, and there is a part of us that is not of this world either. If we trust that part of us, we will be able to find deeper joys in the future and beyond this world when we approach our death sleep.

The life of a Christ follower is a difficult one. It is one of trying to shine in the midst of darkness. Christ himself suffered greatly on the cross. He knew the agony and pain of human suffering and humiliation. But without his death, there could not have been any resurrection.

Simply put, we have a difficult planet to be on, but we do not have to complain about how difficult it is here. We will all know pain, suffering, and death, but we also have the potential to soar above the mundane difficulties of this world and find higher frequencies of truth and proximity to the divine. We have a unique opportunity here to rise above our limitations and show the true mettle of our faith in ways that are not an option for every being in the universe.

Most of all, we must remember that Jesus Christ came to give us a blueprint so that we may know that each of us is worthy of Heaven and eternal life. If we simply follow the path that Christ has laid before us, we will be able to fully realize our spiritual development to the highest potential ever possible.

Life is a Vapor that Vanishes at Dawn

In the New Testament Epistle from James, Jesus' brother, James writes in chapter 4, verses 14 and 15: Whereas ye know not what shall be on the morrow. For what is your life? It is even a vapor, that appeareth for a little time, and then vanisheth away. For that ye ought to say, If the Lord will, we shall live, and do this, or that.

Many early Christians had the same kinds of questions and problems that are familiar to us even today. People were spending their time worrying about building up their treasures, concerning themselves with the ways of this world, and getting lost in unimportant things that did not point to Christ or toward goodness and the purpose of having a fulfilling life on Earth.

James felt that it was necessary to remind people that all that is given to us is the opportunity to trust in God and that the time in which we have to do that is rather a brief one. James compares human life to a vapor that appears briefly and then vanishes away. It is as true today as it was for the original audience that James was writing to.

The point in sharing this is to simply say, that even if you live to be 100, this is still just a blink of an eye in consideration of the time that the universe has been in existence. Even more, it is literally immeasurable when you look at the scope of all eternity.

...We shall not all sleep, but we shall all be changed, in a moment, in the twinkling of an eye... – Corinthians 15:51

No one knows the day or the hour that they will be called back home to Heaven. Death sleep comes for us all and is something that we cannot control. Each moment of each day may be our last. Even babies and young children, unfortunately, die before they can experience much of life. Teenagers and young adults on the brink of discovering their life's purpose can be here one day and gone the next. Life expectancy may be longer now than it was in Jesus' day, but the truth is, the randomness of death is just around the corner for each of us.

It is just as James writes. Life is short and it vanishes soon and without warning. No one knows which day will be their last, so we need to work on developing the breadth of our experience, which means making the most out of each day. We need to always remember this brevity and uncertainty, and the dangerous combination they provide. Doing so is the prescription to cure the common ailment of procrastination.

Too often, we put off doing something for tomorrow that we could do today. We think we will always have more time until we realize we do not. Why not make the most of the day so that the future can be known instead of relegated to mere chance? The better we plan for this day, the more enjoyable the next one will be.

None of us will be perfect, and that is okay. God does not ask for us to be perfect. God does, however, ask for our faith and our trust in Him, and if we work to strive to be better each day, then we have the opportunity to go deeper in our faith and trust in God. It doesn't matter if we are given 20 years or 100; each day is a chance to trust more in God than the day before.

Ultimately, it is inevitable. One day each one of us will pass from this life to the next. In light of this, there are scriptures, like Ecclesiastes that invite us to eat, drink, and be merry, but whatever we do, may it all bring glory to our God. All of our actions should be for the glory of our Creator.

None of us did anything to bring ourselves into this life. Our parents brought us here, and our God created the conditions of living that made it possible. Our God gave us a soul when we made the choice to trust in Him and have faith. If we did nothing to bring about this existence, what makes us think that we are the center of the story? God is the center of the story. As 1 Corinthians 6:19-20 reads: "Don't you realize that your body is the temple of the Holy Spirit, who lives in you and was given to you by God? You do not belong to yourself, for God bought you at a high price. So, you must honor God with your body."

Unfortunately, the difficulties of this particular planet can make it hard for us to put God first. We have to have food and shelter and to do that, we have to work, which often takes most of each day. God, Christ, and the Angels know quite well how difficult it can be for those on Earth to break away from the daily grind because of this. These constructs of constant work and distraction from Christ are part of the system of obscurity created by Lucifer and Satan in his ruling of this earthly kingdom.

Extra Grace and Mercy offered by our Creator to Earthlings

God is aware of Earthly problems, however, and so He provides extra grace to every human. This grace is a way of understanding and patience. It does not look like God interfering with human free will. Even in the difficulties of this world, and with the Creator's grace and mercy, we are still required to take the first step and to direct that step toward God and not away from Christ. Through prayer, meditation, or time with a devotional, we offer the intention to connect with Christ and become closer to God.

An enlightened being once said, "Take a single step closer to me, and I will take 10,000 steps toward you." I couldn't agree more. God desires you so badly and wants nothing more than to be in a relationship with you and see your spirit deepen, your soul thrive, your vibrations yield higher frequencies, and, ultimately, see you come to Heaven and join the heavenly body of God. All of this, though, is secondary to the truth that God gives you free will. As much as God desires all of that for you, God will not break the rules of existence to make them happen. You must take the initiative. Knowing that tomorrow is not promised, you should truly take that initiative today.

No one knows the time when this world will come to an end. Many prophets have come and gone and made their predictions about the Day of Judgement. They have used false equations and have been impure in their intentions most of the time.

That being said, it is clear that the time for harvest is coming to Earth. Without knowing the exact date or time, it can still be abundantly apparent that the Earth is ripening and the time for harvest is soon. This is discussed elsewhere in greater detail, but for the purposes of this chapter, let us focus on the fact that life as a whole is short, and life on Earth is particularly fragile, as it may curtain at any time.

Each one of us is responsible for the time given to us, and we have the chance to use our time wisely so that we can know Christ and God and decide today to follow and trust in Christ. If you make the decision today, God will know what is in your heart. If you truly believe and truly have faith in Christ, you will have a soul the moment God becomes aware of it.

Last shall be the First

Jesus speaks in the Gospel of Matthew 20:16 and tells his listeners, "So the last shall be first, and the first last." While there are many ways that humans have interpreted this scripture over the past two millennia, the variations depend on the spiritual maturity and the mind filters available to the individual who is reading the text.

With the knowledge that we now have, I believe Christ is telling us that while Earth may appear to be last, that does not mean that we cannot be the first in our spiritual pursuits. Here on Earth, we have the opportunity to accumulate spiritual gifts through good deeds and service work and through a deepening relationship with Christ, God, and the Heavens.

To most beings on the outside looking in, the people who are stuck on Earth are considered the last among all beings. But God, through Christ, shows us the way that we can be the first in the following realm if we do all that God gives us the opportunity to do here.

When it is time for the harvest, your gifts might well propel you to much higher levels of Heaven than even angels in Heaven. Compare this to the many angels who are working on lower levels of Heaven. It is good and right that they are in Heaven, to be sure, but we, humans, on Earth might be the last to reach Heaven, but we can become the first to get closer to Christ and God, the Paradise Father.

Even Angels in Heaven stand in awe of Humans on Earth. The darkness that surrounds us day in and day out and how our human spirit breaks through the dark tentacles, makes Angels bow in reverence to the Human species. Only if you can see this sight, you will truly appreciate the value of Human birth.

Let us, then, not squander the opportunities bestowed upon us, and instead be sure to live this hard life with the promise and the hope of the bright light and the greater future that lies beyond us. The next time you are surrounded by chaos and darkness, remember that Christ has given you the blueprint of how to turn the situation around. You may feel like you are in the last row right now, but if you stay in your course, you can be first to God.

Conclusion

The Earth is the greatest 3D classroom there is. This is the great School of Life. Earthly experiences place you in learning conditions to reveal the states of your own Godhead of goodness. We are born on this great Earth with God's divine spark of life. Each one of us is unique and created for a purpose. Remember the entire universe is working in a conspiracy for your growth.

We are required to learn the great laws of creation and to trust and have faith in God and Heaven. For those who seek higher levels of consciousness and devotion to be of service to the Almighty Father in the Kingdom of Heaven, the most difficult "pass" carries with it a great reward as well.

We can attend classes, complete the exams, and join school teams, but if the inner knowledge and understanding aren't developed and retained, there will be repercussions. For it is finding within the inner Kingdom of righteousness in your relationship to God that we not only graduate, but the successful citizens of God's Kingdom reign here on this Earth as well as enter into the Kingdom of Heaven and its glories

The chapters of this book have demonstrated that the Kingdom of Heaven belongs to God and His children, and the only way to get to God and His Kingdom is through Faith and Trust in God/Christ. All elements of Heaven then become accessed from this connection.

When you walk on this path, you may feel alone at some parts of the journey but don't be surprised if there are many teachers that appear to assist you at each step. You are never alone. When you are ready for the next step, your new teacher arrives. This guidance becomes a common process and while at times you may feel like you are a dry well with no ounce of water in sight except for the stinging tears that may drop from a sorrow-filled heart due to obstacles that may challenge the very essence of you who you are, these are the steps and stages that will lead you to the fountain of knowledge. They will appear and guide you to the eternal ocean of love and connection to a Kingdom that is, always has been, and will always be yours as a child of God. Through this experience, the teachers appear and change as you grow through the different levels of evolution. Each moment grants us the opportunity to receive lessons and inspiration in our evolutionary steps on this earthly plane and with the appreciation of our physical vessel that takes us through this journey.

It is important to note that most Humans evolve unconsciously. In other words, you may neither have a conscious recollection of your teachers or guides and what tests you have passed, nor what levels you have achieved in the Heavens or what treasures you have achieved in Heavens. Very few have a conscious recollection. I am fortunate enough to go through a conscious growth process.

The only window into the intricate layers and stories of our consciousness may be found in our sleep. If you pay close attention to your dreams, visions, and your intuition, you may be able to get a good sense of where you stand in your growth process. It has been said that dreams are a window to one's soul and for all intents and purposes, no one knows your soul except yourself and God. There truly is no end to the amount of experience and growth that one has in ability and opportunity in the Heavens and on this Earth to get there. Only your free will and your devotional desire are the prerequisites to the fate that is yours for the taking when you answer the call of your inner Kingdom.

Each person reading this book has the potential to take what they have learned here and really use it to better themselves, improve their chances of obtaining a soul, and make sure that their soul reaches the highest Heaven possible.

There are no limits to this knowledge or the number of people who can benefit from it. If you are reading this, and you believe someone else can learn from it, please share this good news with them in the hopes that they may one day also attain a heavenly form.

Hopefully, by now, you have learned how to shift the old religious frameworks away from exclusion and harmful spirituality, and toward openness and a fruitful faith that will yield a graduation from this difficult life here on Earth, propelling you into the heavenly kingdoms.

Don't worry if you aren't perfect or if you don't have the best relationship with Christ. You will have the chance to improve yourself every day, and if you choose to do that hard work, I promise that you will see the results of your labors, your studying, and your faith and trust in God.

Even if you do not see this world getting any easier, remember that your reward will not be here, but as your being transfers its existence beyond this world and into the heavenly realms, you need to realize that is the real home for each of us.

I believe these pages have helped in some way to make the mystery of heaven a bit less of a mystery. I hope you can now believe that Heaven is worth it and is accessible to all of us.

And when you do make that metamorphosis, and I hope that you do, Christ will welcome you in with the familiar saying, "Well done, my good and faithful servant,", Welcome to Heaven.

Thank You

I want to thank you personally for reading this book.

have poured my Heart and Soul into these pages. I hope you have gained some valuable insights from the information presented. Please consider leaving your valuable review. Your review and feedback are important to me. Thank you so much.

One Click Review:

https://www.amazon.com/review/create-review?&asin=B0C9N358YB

or please scan to leave your Review:

PREVIEW CHAPTER FROM BOOK 2 OF SERIES
WELCOME TO HEAVEN. YOUR FAMILY, MARRIAGE,
SEX, WORK

Chapter 7. What does your life in Heaven look like?

Understanding Heaven and its welcoming doors doesn't take much when we gather all the facts around us and contemplate the Kingdom with a gracious heart. While we can sift through the passages of the Bible and attempt to frame this glorious place from our own limited human awareness and consciousness, gathering these pieces of understanding here with the main goal of analyzing and sharing in this wisdom is based on my understanding of the scriptures, research, and personal experiences.

There is enough knowledge to back up our understanding of Heaven and know what we can expect to experience. Even Christ did not give many details of what life in Heaven looks like, and this gave rise to a lot of speculation among theologians. If you're like me, and due to the number of questions and curiosity that leads you to consider yourself as "a heavenly brat" in a literal sense, try to give yourself a break. God understands the limitations of our human mind and the curiosity of knowledge it seeks.

Many years ago, when I was in the deep valleys of despair and I dived into an intense study of spiritual and religious matters, I heard God ask me if I needed some advice. Shockingly, yet not so surprisingly, I listened and knew it was the voice of God. At the time, I felt depressed and fed up with everything in life, and out of anger, I shouted in anger, "I don't want your advice. I want a Million dollars NOW!" God burst out laughing so loud, He knew it was my ego talking. Who said God does not have a sense of humor?

When speaking with God, you certainly aren't messing around with just anyone. Not only does this experience stick with me until this day, but it's also a reminder that God connects on a personal level, and loves humor and laughter. To this day, I'm still living and working a 9-5 job on a monthly paycheck. With this in mind and as you continue reading this chapter, it's most important to remember that God works in His own time and meets you at the level of your consciousness. God and Heavenly beings do not give in to your ego. If you can accept this, then I believe you may have come that little bit closer to accessing the secret elixir of life- it's essentially what's found in your heart and your relationship with God. This, combined with the knowledge that all of Heaven, including God, Christ, and the angels, love humor and want to laugh, sing, and dance and live life fully, abundantly, and worship the Creator with joy and not out of compulsion.

While you may consider the incessant questioning of the topic of Heaven annoys the best of the Angels within the Heavenly Kingdom, we have a right to postulate, speculate, and with the most fervent inquisition, imagine what the Heavenly Kingdom might be like in all of its glorious details. After all, if this is the place we are destined to go, it makes sense that we would like to know more about it. This chapter is for those who want to try and satisfy their curiosity about what awaits them in their daily life in the eternal Kingdom or at least in the first levels of Heaven. Regardless of this chapter's speculation, it is with an innocent heart I attempt to describe this place that holds so much wonder in our hearts, but without getting too caught up in the nitty-gritty details of Heaven and life. When we place our trust, hope, and faith in Christ, we know we are in good hands. Everything is in the proper place, and we'll arrive at the proper time.

Okay, we are in Heaven! Now What?

The mystery of God never ceases to amaze me. For those with abiding faith who trust and believe in the magnificence of the Father, our Creator, surely Heaven is not disappointing. We have been told that Heaven is worth it. There's eternal bliss, life is eternal, there's peace and joy, and there are countless Angels beyond our imaginations that make it worth living this earthly life and dying for. The Kingdom of

Heaven is an eternal journey, and it's for the believers and seekers of righteousness that it awaits. As it is written, "What no eye has seen, nor ear heard, nor the heart of man imagined, what God has prepared for those who love him" (New International Version, 2011. 1 Corinthians. 2:9). However, we can't truly know this place without having faith and a love for the God who has created us. The burden of life can be pressing upon our earthly soul, but as we endure its lessons and the crosses that we have to carry in this life, Heaven will surely release us from these earthly bonds. It claims in Revelation, "He will wipe away every tear from their eyes, and death shall be no more, neither shall there be mourning, nor crying, nor pain anymore, for the former things have passed away" (English Standard Version, 1971 Revelation. 21:4) The gates of Heaven are waiting for us, and needless to say, there are many questions that can influence our perceptions and hope. This chapter seeks to explain some of them and attempt to answer the question, what does Heaven actually look like?

Communication

Living in paradise means that you will be with other souls in the Kingdom of Heaven. Certainly, joy and heavenly laughter exist when you get through those pearly gates, but needless to say, there will be a transition time required. In this process of transitory evolution, there will be a new way of thinking and being, including how you communicate. We may not need to have the latest iPhone or rely on GPS to get to go somewhere or connect with those we love in the heavenly realm. Communicating with Christ, God, and the Heavenly angels probably won't rely on text or Messenger services. Communication will be different than it ever has been known to you before. While our electronic devices are necessary and greatly appreciated in this mortal plane, when you pass through Heaven's doors, the new ways to understand and communicate with others will be at the next level too. This occurs upon the understanding and realization that your Soul body has many extra senses that will open up and evolve. You will have your own messenger services, and among them is telepathy, which is known as being able to read others' thoughts. I believe telepathy will be the general method of communication in Heaven. Also, being there at the right time and place may not be a random event anymore but something that happens frequently and without surprise. Because this is just how things operate on a daily basis in this Kingdom of God's Creation.

Your work in Heaven

In terms of work and making a living, some people predict that Heaven can be seen as a forever retirement home. Unlike Earth, there is no struggle to survive, and getting a 9-to-5 job to pay the mortgage is not something that will be a requirement for you. When we leave this mortal plane, we enter a dimension and a perpetual state of safety and security that only God's Kingdom can provide. Each being has all that is needed, including food, clothing, and shelter. While this may be difficult to imagine at this time in your life for some of you. All beings will be in service to one another and many levels to the Kingdom of Heaven, not only house choruses and multitudes of angels, of which you will be one, but you will be a part of His grand symphony and community of children.

What you will do on a daily basis is up to you. There are also angels whose sole purpose is to understand what your desires are and help you to find your passions or your desires. You will choose what you want to do, and no one can enforce anything on you. However, having a mindset based in goodness and righteousness also supports your state of consciousness that is focused on prayer and devotion to Christ and God the Father. This will neither be affected by distractions after a long day of hard work at your day job nor by watching the latest series of interesting on your cable network that may be a part of your daily routine here. You and God's angels will end up choosing that which is suitable for you and ready for you at any given moment.

The profession you choose depends on your Soul purpose, your skills, and your aspirations. No one will enforce what you must do. It can be considered as voluntary work that you enjoy doing and want to learn and contribute. The professions can be any in the realms of music, science, leadership positions, art, technology, spiritual teaching…etc. Heaven is much more dynamic and has more opportunities than Earth life presents. On Earth, most of us have a 9 to 5 job to pay for bills, to be able to put food on the table, and general family maintenance. In Heaven, all basics are met, and there is no struggle for survival.

Temples in Heaven

It may seem strange that once you get to Heaven, you'll still be praying. I mean, isn't that what life is on earth for? Once you get past those gates, you've made it, right? The heart and soul of a believer in God means that this eternal love and devotion never ceases. Heaven provides the perfect place for more devotional practice. As we know, Heaven houses many rooms, mansions, and people, the places of worship will be everywhere, and the practice of spirituality will still exist in Heaven. Many authors refer to these temples as Morontia temples and there are many.

All angels worship God and Christ, and when you get there, there won't be much difference. However, there are spiritual leaders, temples to visit, and schools of thought that teach about creation and different levels of Heaven, Christ, and God, while you're there. Here on earth, many people take pilgrimages to learn about God and become closer to Him. Likewise, in Heaven, the communities and people will all be focused on the same principles of worship, where spiritual closeness to divine oneness and evolution is often together or in groups where learning and growth are easily facilitated.

The Heavenly Community

It's when people gather in the community that we can share and delight in the teaching of Christ more profoundly. Knowing more people will be praying and celebrating Christ and the Kingdom of Heaven together, it's easy to imagine your arrival in the Heavenly community will indeed add to the fanfare. In previous chapters, we have addressed the multitude of people who will be there, and all of them bear differences yet possess the same devotion. The Bible also acknowledges that there is a "great multitude" of people who exist in Heaven. "After this, I looked, and behold a great multitude that no one could number, from every nation, from all tribes and peoples and languages, standing before the throne and before the Lamb, clothed in white robes, with palm branches in their hands" (New International Version, 2011,). To envision such a glorious uniting of world nations, without borders in the Kingdom of Heaven, is thrilling and sublime. Heaven will truly house the believers of the Creator of the world as One in peace and unity.

Money in Heaven

There is no monetary system in heaven. Your richness is not measured by your bank balance or your possessions. Sorry, Jeff Bezos, Bill Gates, Elon. Your true wealth is your Soul experiences, the richness of love, and the good intentions you carry. You will be your soul-like. The radiance you emit will display your inner glory. Similar to the barter system people exchange favors for each other, but there is no concept of money transactions.

Elements of Creation in Heaven

In our material world all of the things we see, feel or touch have a chemical composition that we have defined in our periodic table (118+ elements). Also, we have five senses touch, sight, hearing, smell, and taste. In heaven the number of elements is much more and more refined, the colors visible are so many more, and senses are not limited to those we know of. Much of this this explained well by the authors of Truthbook.

Pain and illness

There is no pain and illness in heaven. There is no pain on earth that heaven cannot heal.

"He will wipe away every tear from their eyes, and death shall be no more, neither shall there be mourning, nor crying, nor pain anymore, for the former things have passed away" (Revelation 21:3-4).

Your Life in Heaven. Family, Marriage, Sex, Work

"No eye has seen, no ear has heard, and no mind has imagined what God has prepared for those who love him." – 1 Corinthians 2:9

Ever wonder what your **life in Heaven will look like after your mortal death**?

Is there **Marriage** in Heaven? Do you have a **Family in Heaven**?

Do you have your **Parents or kids or your siblings** in Heaven?

Do you have **Sexual intercourse** in Heaven?

And what do you do all day? Is there a **daily Job**? Oh. And will you meet your **deceased family members**, friends, and relatives?

These are questions that curious minds like me ask. You will find **authoritative un-speculated** answers here.

PREVIEW FROM BOOK - LUCIFER REBELLION BOOK1: CHRIST VS SATAN-FINAL BATTLE FOR EARTH HAS BEGUN

Chapter 10: Clarion Call from GOD to all Angels in Heaven

"What takes place on Earth is very important to Heaven." - Trinity Royal

In the previous chapters, you've learned about the spiritual forces at play throughout history and in the world right now. Even though they are unknown to the vast majority of humanity, you have chosen to open your eyes and discover how they have been and are influencing you and everyone around you. As Morpheus would say, You have taken the red pill.

With the knowledge you now possess, it is time to move on to more advanced topics where you will gain significantly more depth of knowledge. While you've learned about the spiritual Matrix, and how Dark-aligned and Light-aligned entities influence Earth–whether by enslaving humans or liberating them, encouraging selfishness rather than altruism, and so on, now you'll see specific instances of these activities–and the rationales behind specific plans launched by both sides in the war– especially centering around Jesus Christ and His teachings.

Why God Needs Your Help

We have seen in the previous chapters that the War came to be centered on planet Earth. Earth is the epicenter of the battle between Dark and Light. What happens here affects the rest of the Universe.

Due to this, the human race has become God's prized possession, and our planet Earth– also called Urantia in higher realms of consciousness–is the site of many of God's most important plans and a storehouse of His most valuable resources. For the purposes of this book, we don't need to go too far into the details of the Universal Father's creative activity, or every one of His agents. Here, we will simply go over the broadest, most basic points of Earth's history you need to know to get a grasp of what you need to do to help the forces of Light.

God's own son "the Son of God" is Christ, who is also the creator of the Universe. Millions of years ago, Christ manipulated many nebulae to form stars, and thus our galaxy, and around one of these stars at the edge of one of these galaxies is the Milky Way. Each galaxy consists of numerous solar systems and planets.

When our Creator created this planet, He noted that there was something special about this little blue orb, it became known as the "seed" planet. The seed planets are considered special as new souls are developed on these kinds of planets. The seed planets are the training ground for young Souls on an evolutionary path. There are very few in number in this part of our galaxy. Christ with the help of Trinity consciousness (God the Universal Father, Eternal, Son, and Infinite Spirit) created the Human species. So we are created in His "likeness" as the scriptures state, making the residents of our planet particularly important for the plans of both God and Satan.

Human beings evolved empathy, compassion, altruism, and especially religious feelings much earlier in our development than was the case for sentient beings in other worlds. As a result, the spiritual energies produced by the development of human souls, whether ascending towards higher consciousness realms as the Light desires or chained down to this lower dimensional consciousness as the Dark desires, far outweigh those produced by even heavenly beings in the universe. Since the war has been at a stalemate in the rest of the Universe for a very long time, with neither Lucifer's forces nor the Light has been able to dislodge the other, Earth has taken center stage as the decisive point. Darkness, unfortunately, has managed to make significant in-roads on our planet and has advanced its plans very far. On the other hand, the Universal Father has plans of his own involving His most powerful agent here: Jesus Christ, whom we shall learn more about in future chapters. This should suffice as an overview of the Universal Father treasures humanity in particular so much.

Effects of the Rebellion

Now, due to Lucifer's rebellion, discussed in previous chapters, God has had a very difficult time reaching out to humanity, protecting and guiding us, despite how highly He valued us. The path for growth toward the Light was growing harder and harder for us, with many obstacles placed in our way. Here are some of the ways Darkness has interfered with us:

- No real religious teachings. There have been many great religions started by enlightened prophets which have been stamped out by the Dark. Humanity has been made to forget these religions and their teachings to delay the growth of many strong souls and prevent knowledge about the great spiritual conflict from spreading widely.

- Manipulation of teachings. Cunning agents of Darkness have manipulated some teachings of religions throughout history–and in the present day–to sow confusion and make it even harder for seekers to attain genuine knowledge of Heaven and higher spiritual realms.

- Over-emphasis on the process: Partially due to machinations from the Dark, but also due to honest mistakes which built up over time, much of humanity has become too focused on ritual–rather than finding their own individual "spark" of God within themselves.

Finally, whereas direct communication with God is possible on higher realms that are more vibrationally attuned to Paradise–the Veil or Matrix which envelopes Earth has cut us off from the Divine in some way. Only if we are very fortunate can some of us access higher realities, and often only in dreams; communion with the Universal Father Himself is very rare, with only the Bestowal of Christ giving us hope (described in the next chapter).

Even so, there are some agents of the Light who have come to Earth to assist us in reaching higher consciousness levels, even if they were not in direct contact with the Divine. Some gods in ancient polytheistic or henotheistic religions were heavenly messengers who came to help Humanity in the evolution process. Also religious figures like Lord Buddha or Lord Krishna, philosophers like Aristotle, Plato, Zeno of Elea, Confucius, and some modern-day personages like Martin Luther King. Some angels even gave inspiration to great inventors and teachers, like Jonas Salk–creator of the polio vaccine, Albert Einstein, and other Nobel Prize winners.

All these people were sent or influenced by the Light to guide mankind towards the climactic event which will occur soon, in the present time we are living in. The Dark has also influenced our world in many ways, both enslaving individual humans, trapping their souls, encouraging the evolution of dark cults, and, teaching other individuals selfish methods of increasing their power and influence. Some Dark agents manifested in this world directly, putting on human disguises, while others merely contacted ordinary people seeking power and subtly guided them into the shadows. Many Dark agents or servants settled as kings, queens, or great and bloody conquerors. Adolf Hitler and Ghenghis Khan are two such examples. Less famously, Dark agents generally tried-and are still trying- to infiltrate large, powerful, centralized governments to control information and how people lived, to ensure as few as possible could ascend. They also manipulate the genetic code of humanity, to cut out strands of DNA carrying Light codes-such as nobler, more altruistic temperaments, higher attunement to spiritual realities, a higher propensity to dream-and so on.

Despite both sides doing their best throughout hundreds of thousands of years, Light was never able to break Dark's grasp on the world, and Dark could never remove every trace of Light from Earth, even as its influence steadily grew.

Thus, the war on Earth was grinding down into a stalemate as well; whatever advantages Dark had would take many, many centuries to come to fruition. Before that can happen, the forces of Light desire to strike a shattering blow against Satan/Lucifer. The fallen Morning Star, cunning as he is, anticipated that, and is attempting to gather his forces for his decisive annihilation of Light on Earth, which will allow him to capture the planet and turn all of the prodigious energy humans produce into his ends.

God's Counterattack

As the situation on Earth is rapidly heating up, the Universal Father focused more and more of His energies and attention on it. About 200,000 years ago, He made a clarion call to all of His angels to focus on humanity and do all they can to uplift the consciousness of this blue orb. God is no fool and made clear to His angelic forces that this would likely be the most difficult mission they had ever attempted ever in their entire existence. God also emphasized to them this struggle was worth it, for He realized how unique and powerful humanity is due to its peculiar evolutionary history, and thus He loves humanity and Earth more than any other place in the Universe. Much of God's focus is on humanity and earth at the present time. This is an absolute fact.

This clarion call rang out wide to all of Heavens and Paradise. The mission was simply to save Humans and Earth. A mission like this was never attempted in the history of creation.

Since this was unique, a vast number of angels had no idea what to expect and did not sign up for the mission. Given the incredible skills, the angels possessed, very many of them could not take it for fear of the unknown. Many were afraid of the struggle and Satan's forces in general and were also uncertain of the outcome. Most have already witnessed the devastation caused by Lucifer's rebellion in the Heavens. After all, such an endeavor had never been attempted before, and no histories existed in the great archives and annals of Heaven that could give any guidance on a war like this. The angels who raised these concerns did not have full faith in the Universal Father's victory, so they chose to sit out the battle and wait and see who would win. Others did not want to limit their consciousness by focusing on one planet in one system in one planet of the vast Universe.

In fairness to these seemingly cowardly angels, fighting Satan's forces on Earth is a truly monumental task. The Matrix surrounding Earth has several characteristics that make things harder for the Light than the Dark.

However, some angels did have faith in God and Christ and said "yes" to this divine mission. There were at least 144,000 of these according to the Holy Bible. These are the angles who have agreed to come into the Matrix and be part of the Matrix, mingle with evolving Human souls, and increase the vibrations of Human consciousness thereby helping God and the cause of light. These angels were known as descended angels. According to a divinely orchestrated plan, these brave angelic souls planted themselves at predetermined strategic points of Human evolution to become teachers, preachers, inventors, gurus, sadhus, scientists..etc. Basically to teach and help evolve Humanity.

Then I looked, and behold, the Lamb was standing on Mount Zion, and with Him one hundred and forty-four thousand, having His name and the name of His Father written on their foreheads. – Revelations 14:1

However life is not all rosy for these brave angels; by being in the Matrix, all of them got caught up in the illusion of the Matrix, and most if not all forgot their divine origins and intermingled with humans over the period of 200,000 years. This has helped to manipulate the DNA of the Human species, thereby evolving the human species faster and closer to God. If Light wins, these brave angels will enjoy all the splendor and accolades they have earned.

The Matrix prevents spiritual beings from heavenly realms from passing into Earth. They are only allowed in if a resident of Earth, within the Matrix itself, specifically asks them to enter. This is called the doctrine of non-interference. Some beings can get around this, but it is extremely rare, and Dark forces like demons and shadow-whisperers more often do this. The great Bestowal of Christ was one exception to this rule in Light's favor. Another exception was the case of 'original seeders,' angels who visited humanity in distant past eons to place Light information in our genomes.

The effects of the Matrix on the development of the soul itself present another obstacle to the cause of Light due to loss of memory. Souls, ignorant as they are, cannot easily coordinate with each other, or angelic beings, and must rely on their internal abilities to evolve, which can be made easier if the bodies to which they are reincarnated possess useful strands of Light-aligned DNA. In this regard, humans possessing these types of DNA should mingle as much as possible with the rest of the human population to spread them far and wide and to future generations, but again, since accumulated knowledge is lost, this is harder to do. Souls must also learn their own lessons, rather than being taught, how to avoid the pitfalls of the Dark, transform Dark energies into Light ones, and enhance the collective consciousness of humanity.

Given all this, you can imagine why God is personally concerned with this war on a single small planet and refuses to give up on the human race. It is extremely important for Him and the Light to win this war, as so many of His strongest angels have already invested so much. In other words, not only are human souls at stake, but Paradise and other types of angels from higher heavenly realms also have vulnerable souls that might be at risk if they lose. Thus, God has a vested interest in you—yes, you! He wants your soul to grow, advance, and improve your spiritual life so you can help in the struggle. This will determine whether Light or Dark wins in the end.

If you like this preview…you will love this book. Get it today

Lucifer Rebellion. Christ vs. Satan – Final Battle for Earth Has Begun

Multiple Award-winning Book

"extraordinary book" "Definitely a five-star read" - [International Review of Books]

Ever wonder **why there is a War between GOD and the Devil?** Ever wonder how the **War in Heaven started or what the Lucifer Rebellion is**?

Ever wonder why War in heaven came to Earth or why darkness still exists on Earth? And why did God send Christ to Earth?

This book explores:

- How and Why did the **war in Heaven start**? How did the War in Heaven come to Earth?

- Why did **God send Christ** to planet Earth? Was it to save Humanity and the Universe?

- What exactly happened during **Christ's First Coming** event? What is expected during the Second Coming event?

Trinity takes us on a **journey beyond time and space** to find the answers to these questions that every believer should know.

Lucifer Rebellion. Christ vs Satan – The Second Coming of Christ

Ever wonder **why there is a War between GOD and Devil?**

Ever wonder how the **War in Heaven started or what Lucifer Rebellion is?** **and why War in Heaven came to Earth** and why darkness still exists on Earth?

This book explores:

- How and Why did the **war in Heaven start**?
- How did the War in Heaven come to Earth?

- Why did **God send Christ** to planet Earth? Was it to save Humanity and the Universe?

- What are the effects of War on Earth and in Heaven?

- What exactly happened during **Christ's First Coming** event?

- What is expected during the Second Coming event?

I invite you to join me on a journey beyond space and time when the Lucifer Rebellion started and the reasons for Christ's First and Second Coming events.

CHRIST & DEMONS - UNSEEN REALMS OF DARKNESS

"The reason the Son of God appeared was to destroy the Devil's work." -1 John 3:8

Is there an **UNSEEN world of Darkness** hidden in front of our eyes?

Ever wonder why **Evil** exists on Earth? Ever wonder how **Satan got to planet Earth** and what exactly is the Dark Empire Agenda?

Ever wonder why Christ chose planet Earth for His great Bestowal?

What is the **agenda of Darkness**? Why do God and Christ let dark forces flourish on Earth? Does God have a plan? What is it?

What are the differences between **Demons, Evil Spirits, and Ghosts**? How does **Selling one's Soul to the devil** happen?

Son of Man becomes Son of God. One Event that Changed the History of the World

Award-Winning Book

"an opportunity for the reader to embark on a journey with Him, feel what He feels"

"A fascinating description and story of how Christ emerged, changed and developed into the highest of holiest beings, second only to God."

"An exceptional and well-written novel without the preaching and pointless prose and verbiage of others of this type"

There is **ONE event** that is the true turning point in the history of Earth. This is not the Birth or

Baptism of Jesus, but it is the **fight with the Devil**

Ever wonder what would have happened to Earth if Christ failed against Satan? This was a real possibility, although it is considered blasphemous to talk about it.

From Suffering to Healing

Scan Me

"I highly recommend this for anyone **who has ever suffered in their lives**, and, in all honesty, who hasn't?"

Why do **bad things happen to good people**?

Why does your **Life journey lead you to suffer?**

The Answer is to Heal You.

Your suffering is the epitome of a **blessing in disguise.** Wrapped in darkness and suffering, it removes the ground from beneath your feet and leaves you fearful, fragile, and devoid of meaning in life.

Most beings that we adore or worship have gone through dark times in their life. This includes Christ, Buddha, Gandhi, Nelson Mandela, Oprah, Abraham Lincoln, etc. This process is necessary as it redefines a person, re-makes one character, and chips away the darkness to bring out the luster of your **Real Self.** This is your **METAMORPHOSIS**.

Award-Winning Book

Our wounds are often the openings into the best and the most beautiful parts of us." -David Richo

Ever wonder **why suffering happens for no known reason...**

Ever wonder **why your Soul is longing**...

Have you ever felt like you have a **splinter in your mind, that does not let you off the hook..**

If so, **you are chosen for a purpose. There is GOD's hand working in your life.**

While there are many reasons people suffer (most are self-made or bad decisions or external in nature); the type of Suffering referred to as the "Dark Night of the Soul" has a clear and definite purpose. ***The purpose is your Soul's growth***.

Your Answers and Healing await. Click on Buy Now.

SOS - Save yOur Soul. What Happens After You Die?

"For what shall it profit a man, if he shall gain the whole world, and lose his own soul?" - Mark 8:36

Ever Wonder **What Happens After You Die**? Is it the end?

What did **Christ** Say about death and life after mortal death?

Is there a way to Save yOur Soul? If so How?

What exactly is **Soul** and **Spirit**, is it just a new age concept? What did Christ Say?

Trinity considered to be one of the bridges between Heaven and Earth, shares general Angelic knowledge. This book explores:

What are the unseen parts of us that make us who we are? What is left behind after Mortal death and what happens to these **unseen parts of us**?

What exactly is **Soul** and **Spirit**, is it just a new age concept? What did Christ Say? Is there a way to Save yOur Soul? If so How? Does Heaven actually exist? Can a ticket to Heaven be guaranteed?

WHAT HAPPENED ON EASTER SATURDAY? 36 HR MYSTERY BETWEEN DEATH AND RESURRECTION

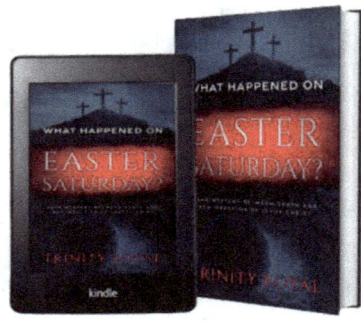

"*A five-star read, absolutely.*"

" **It stands to reason that Saturday was a critical time for Him**"

"I highly recommend this incredible book as it takes the reader through both the physical and spiritual journey of Him as he underwent His transformation. ***A five-star read, absolutely***."

"I for one never really thought about that Saturday, so for me **it was a riveting experience**, learning about that previously overlooked time."

Ever wonder **what happened when Christ was inside the Tomb for 36 hrs** between death and resurrection?

Ever wonder **what body did Christ have after Resurrection**? and why the **resurrection process take 3 days?** why not 1-day or 2-days?

FREE BOOKS TO OUR READERS

War in Heaven came to Earth. Satan Rebellion:

https://dl.bookfunnel.com/ea12ys3dmk

Your Life in Heaven:

https://dl.bookfunnel.com/vg451qpuzs

REFERENCES

Thomas Moore Quotes. (n.d.). *Thomas Moore Quotes.* BrainyQuote. www.brainyquote.com/quotes/thomas_moore_386766

Anderson, Carla. (May, 2010). *Golden Keys to Achieving Ascension - God Equals Man Minus Ego.* Ezine Articles. https://ezinearticles.com/?Golden-Keys-to-Achieving-Ascension---3---God-Equals-Man-Minus-Ego&id=4226719

(n.a). (December, 2022). *Buddhism.* Encyclopedia of Buddhism. https://encyclopediaofbuddhism.org/wiki/Buddhism

Cherry, Kendra. (October, 2022). *What is Consciousness?* Very Well Mind. https://www.verywellmind.com/what-is-consciousness-2795922

(n.a.). (2023). *Concept of Heaven and Hell According to the Quran.* Quran Reading.

http://www.quranreading.com/blog/concept-of-heaven-and-hell-according-to-islam/

Ehrman, Bart. (May, 2020). *What Jesus Really Said About Heaven and Hell.* TIME. https://time.com/5822598/jesus-really-said-heaven-hell/

Guyon, Madame. (1980). *Experiencing the Depths of Jesus Christ.* (Second Edition). Christian Books.

(n.a.). (January, 2022). How To Get to Heaven - What Are the Ideas of Different Religions. Got Questions. https://www.gotquestions.org/how-to-get-to-heaven.html

Kempis, Thomas. (1934). *The Imitation of Christ.* The Penguin Classics.

King James Bible. (2017). King James Bible Online. https://www.kingjamesbibleonline.org/ (Original work published 1769)

www.truthbook.com

(n.a.). (2007). *Heaven and Hell, According to Various Religions.* Neatorama. https://www.neatorama.com/2007/03/23/heaven-and-hell-according-to-various-religions/

New International Version. (1973). Bible Study Tools. https://www.biblestudytools.com/niv/

New King James Bible. (1982). King James Bible Online. https://www.kingjamesbibleonline.org/new-features.php

Pines, Shlomo. (2022). Judaism. Britannica. https://www.britannica.com/topic/Judaism

(n.a.). (2022). *Quotes from Upanishads.* Reflect and Respond. https://reflectandrespond.com/powerful-100-quotes-from-upanishads/

Shelton, Jacob. (September, 2021). *15 Eerie Details and Theories About the Montauk Project and Camp Hero.* Ranker. https://www.ranker.com/list/facts-about-time-travel-and-the-montauk-project/jacob-shelton

Starr, Mirabai. (2013). *Saint Teresa of Avila - Passionate Mystic.* Sounds True, Inc.

(n.a.). (January, 2017). *21 Grams Experiment.* Wikipedia. https://en.wikipedia.org/wiki/21_grams_experiment#:~:text=Despite%20its%20rejection%20 within%20the,that%20it%20weighs%2021%20grams.

(n.a.). (n.d.). *The Urantia Book.* Urantia. https://www.urantia.org/urantia-book-standardized/foreword#U0_0_5

Wilson, Jim. (2013). *Schumann Resonance.* NASA.

About Author

Trinity is a multi-award-winning author and a spiritual warrior. While life might not always work out according to plan, Trinity was able to take valuable lessons from each new experience. Trinity grew and developed and now shares a passion for enlightening others on spiritual knowledge in the hopes of closing the gap between Heaven and Earth. Trinity's writings reflect the depths of a passion and desire to connect with everyone seeking spiritual growth and education.

You can learn more at

www.RocketshipPath2God.com or @

https://www.facebook.com/TrinityRoyalBooks

www.ingramcontent.com/pod-product-compliance
Lightning Source LLC
Chambersburg PA
CBHW072115050526
44107CB00098BA/191